CATHOLIC SPIRITUALITY
AND THE HISTORY OF RELIGIONS

Catholic Spirituality in Global Perspective

Volume 1
CHRISTIAN UNIQUENESS AND CATHOLIC SPIRITUALITY

Volume 2
CATHOLIC SPIRITUALITY AND THE HISTORY OF RELIGIONS

Catholic Spirituality and the History of Religions

Denise Lardner Carmody
and
John Tully Carmody

PAULIST PRESS
New York ◇ Mahwah

Library of Congress Cataloging-in-Publication Data

Carmody, Denise Lardner, 1935–
    Catholic spirituality and the history of religions/Denise Lardner Car-
mody and John Tully Carmody.
        p.   cm.—(Catholic spirituality in global perspective; v. 2)
    Includes bibliographical references and index.
    ISBN 0-8091-3285-0
    1. Religions.   2. Spirituality—Catholic Church.   I. Carmody, John,
1939–   II. Title.   III. Series.
BL80.2.C335   1991
232—dc20   91-27683
                                                                    CIP

Published by Paulist Press
997 Macarthur Boulevard
Mahwah, New Jersey 07430

Printed and bound in the
United States of America

Contents

For Tom Peterson

Preface to the Series

Our hope for the volumes that appear in *Catholic Spirituality in Global Perspective* is to place at the service of all Christians interested in the significance of the world religions for their own faith the fruits of recent work on both the world religions and Christian spirituality. In stressing spirituality, rather than theology, we have taken aim at the existential, personal implications of the current encounter between Christians and people of other faiths. In stressing the catholic dimension of the Christian tradition, we have tried to acknowledge the limitations of our own religious formation.

Although the series is not intended as a work of apologetics, it does spring from a sense that the Christ met in prayer and social service is often undervalued in interreligious dialogue. Inasmuch as we believe this Christ to be the best interpretation of human existence, much of our reflection revolves around how Christians may appropriate the riches of other traditions without threatening the primacy of the Lord loved by the saints and shining from the pages of the New Testament as *the* great event of history. Our intent is certainly not to be fideists, closed to the enrichments and challenges presented by new times, unwilling to reason about the traditional Christian positions. But it is to ease the way of Christian believers to assimilate the experience of non-Christians into their own prayer and service of Christ. The truth we strive to honor is twofold: the holiness manifested outside of institutional Christianity, and the conviction of Christian tradition that Jesus Christ is the definitive savior.

We owe special thanks to Kevin Lynch, C.S.P., and Larry Boadt, C.S.P., of Paulist Press for welcoming this openended project.

Preface

This book is the second volume in our open-ended series dealing with Catholic spirituality in a global culture. Here the topic is what Christians can gain from studying the history of religions—humanity's overall struggle to find its way in a mysterious world. As will become apparent, our focus in this book is not academic. Though we draw on scholarship concerning various non-Christian traditions, our intent is always to offer nourishment to people already intrigued with Christ and satisfied that he points out their way.

Spirituality, as we conceive of it, may be studied academically, but such study is quite secondary to practice. It is what people who pray and labor for social justice make of our offerings that will be their best test. So we have aimed for reflections and language that might stimulate practitioners of Christian spirituality to new angles of vision, perhaps even to new emphases in praxis. Because we believe that the one God revealed in Christ has operated in every corner of the world, in every chamber of the human heart, we think that any lovely insight, wherever nurtured, can enter into the Christian's treasury. Our hope, then, is that by the end of this volume readers will have expanded their sense of the blessings and goodness of God, of the beauty of the incarnate Word, and of the intimacy of the Holy Spirit.

Chapter 1

Introduction

The History of Religions

During the twentieth century academic studies of religion have proliferated. Many of these studies, undertaken in secular universities, have not been theological. That is to say, they have prescinded from faith-commitment to a given religion as a personal pathway through life. In a scholarly detachment similar to that attempted by professors of history or literature, university professors of religion have studied the rise of Buddhist philosophy, or the development of Muslim law, or Taoist rites for exorcising a person possessed by demons. The assumption has been that knowledge of such topics is good in itself, and that simply by increasing understanding of religious behavior or thought scholars have contributed significantly to a deeper appreciation of human nature.

Theologians need have no quarrel with such detached scholarship. On its own terms, it does render a significant service. Indeed, if we group the various secular approaches to the religious experience of humankind under the designation "the history of religions," as many of the most influential university scholars would find congenial, we can say that the history of religions has opened new horizons in which the persistence of humanity's fascination with sacredness and divinity becomes more impressive than many theologians have appreciated. Committed to their own particular religious tradition, Christian, Jewish, Muslim, or other, theologians have often failed to appreciate how much searching for God, and apparent finding of God, has gone on outside the borders of their own particular tradition. Relatedly, they have often failed to articulate an adequate view of how their own God has related to the religious activity of outsiders. So the increasing accomplishments

3

of the history of religions have tended to force theologians to be less provincial. As it becomes more and more obvious that divinity has not left itself without witness anywhere (Acts 14:17), theologians of all traditions are tending to take a closer look at the ways and thoughts of outsiders.

For our purposes, the history of religions beckons as a considerable challenge and stimulus to Catholic spirituality. As Catholic theologians learn more about the accomplishments of Hindus and Buddhists, Muslims and Jews, Confucians and Taoists, and many others, they can realize that the grace of their God has been even more magnanimous than they had previously appreciated. Specifically they can realize that holiness cuts across religious borders, and that in most locales God has produced saints capable of witnessing to the primacy of the divine goodness. Our goal in this book is to elaborate some of the data bearing on such realizations. By surveying some of the findings of recent studies in the history of religions that bear on the spiritual experience of non-Christians, we hope to concretize the thesis that the God revealed in Jesus Christ has been at work everywhere, encouraging people to be their better selves—encouraging them finally to surrender themselves to the divine mystery.

So we are approaching the history of religions as a friendly, fertile field, ripe for theological reflection. The questions we raise boil down to the following: "What do these reports suggest about the Christian God, and how may they enrich Christians' practice of their own faith?" Many scholars working in the history of religions would find such a question completely legitimate, but some would either have no interest in it or would be antagonistic. The scholars having no difficulty with the prospect of theologians trying to appropriate the wisdom of other traditions for their own faith realize that the history of religions is not itself a religion. In other words, they realize that detached scholarship cannot substitute for personal commitment, because in the final analysis the mysteriousness of human existence forces all people to acts of faith—ways of coping with the terrors of evil and death, as well as with the splendors of love and creativity. The question that always remains after detached scholarship, no matter how brilliant, is, "What am I going to do about this? How does it square with the worldview I have developed to make my own life meaningful?" Inasmuch as this question is not only legitimate but a matter of moral obligation (because unless one asks it of significant new information one is not honoring the claims that such data make on one's conscience), no healthy scholar objects to it. Indeed, all healthy scholars, especially those who are also teachers, want those receiving their work to be serious and personal about it in precisely this way.

But some scholars working at the history of religions are alienated from theology and personal faith. Whether for good reasons (the inadequacies in the religious traditions to which they were exposed during their formative years) or bad (a fear of the demands that a tradition makes, when one takes it fully seriously, as a personal, existential pathway), such scholars resent the tendency of theologians (people trying to correlate new data with a tradition to which they are personally committed) to seek correlations or appropriations of their work. They wish, for example, that Catholic theologians would keep their hands off studies of Hindu yoga or Muslim ritual. They fear that the pristine, clean quality of their work, which has profited from scholarly detachment, will lose out to smudgy efforts to make it profit Catholic (or Protestant, or Orthodox, or Jewish) faith. Indeed, they fear that the theologians' desire to square findings from the history of religions with given views of God's grace or human sinfulness will distort such findings from the outset, putting the theologian in a frame of mind that makes it impossible to hear what outsiders are really saying. A prejudgment that yoga or ritual or views of ultimate reality have to fit some orthodoxy (in our case Catholic) will cause the theologians to tilt the data, or deny the interpretation of the experience in question that the people who had it themselves put forward.

These are serious worries, and theologians ought to take them seriously. There is a danger of premature appropriation, of not listening carefully, of imposing one's own categories on other people's experiences in ways that render it unrecognizable to them. On the other hand, if theologians, or ordinary people of faith, learn about interesting, challenging achievements of other religious traditions, they are bound to wonder how such achievements relate to their own faith, what they imply for their own commitment to Christ or Torah or the Qur'an. In our case, Christ, as venerated by the Catholic Christian tradition, is the partner to such a correlation, and Christ does have more authority than any data received from the outside, because Christ is the treasure on which our tradition has set its heart. Still, we understand Christ to be the truth, as well as the way and the life, so we cannot think that any distortion of data received from the outside (testimony of non-Christians about their religious experience) would honor him. Indeed, one of the most salutary results of Christians' immersion in interreligious dialogue recently has been a humbling of unthinking Christian claims to exclusive rights concerning either revelation or salvation.[1]

Christians have had to admit that the arena of God's activity has been much larger than what has gone on in their own church or through their own theological categories. The striking holiness and good faith of many outsiders argue that they must have contacted God, or been moved by God, with no obvious dependence on either Christ or the Christian church. Thus God must have purposes and ways that exceed those usually stressed in Christian circles. The divine mystery must be much richer than what Christians, theologians and laity alike, have tended to realize. In our opinion, this humbling is all to the good for Christian spirituality. Just as John the Baptist thought that he ought to decrease in stature and Jesus increase (Jn 3:30), so the spiritual categories that Catholics have developed to date ought to decrease in self-importance or self-assurance, when it becomes clear that they cannot contain or render fully appreciatively the good effects of God's Spirit in outsiders' hearts. Ideally this humility would go hand in hand with a great gratitude for these further revelations of the divine bounty, and with a willingness to let the riches of outsiders challenge Christian assumptions, especially those that have become smug and self-serving. That is one of our main hopes in launching both this particular volume and our whole series of inquiries into the future of Catholic spirituality in light of today's global consciousness.

Catholic Spirituality

If we have suggested what "the history of religions" connotes in this book and why reflecting on its implications could be useful, it remains to suggest what "Catholic spirituality" connotes. First, it connotes the Christian tradition in which we authors grew up and so know most personally. Second, we hope that it does not connote something divisive, unecumenical, but rather a large-hearted view of all Christian experience—anything useful to the "great church" that from earliest times sought to be a comprehensive community welcoming all people interested in loving the Father of Jesus Christ. Thus, much that we assume to be Catholic will be completely congenial and familiar to

Protestants and Eastern Orthodox. Third, we take Catholic spirituality to be the existential face of a faith indebted to Roman authorities but never indentured to them. Living faith always escapes tidy controls. Neither church officials nor theologians can dictate how the Spirit of God will choose to move in people's hearts. At their best, both church officials and theologians want mainly to serve and second the movements of the Spirit, realizing that when they do not serve the Spirit they produce only dead letters. So, our sense of "Catholic spirituality" draws more from the saints and current reports on ways that Christians are vivifying their faith, are actually seeking and finding God, than from decrees of either church officials or mainstream theologians. Without denying the value of the services that both officials and theologians can offer, we are more interested in the potential that study of other traditions and dialogue with other traditions offer Christians trying to love their God and neighbors much better.

Christian spirituality, which at most points is interchangeable with Catholic spirituality, knows instinctively that prayer, both individual and communal, is richer than any liturgical theology, let alone than any rubrics. It knows that the law of faith follows from the law of prayer, and that the law of prayer is nothing less than the free dispositions of the Holy Spirit. Something parallel holds for the second major concern of Christian spirituality, action to improve the world, to increase social justice. The most creative expressions of Christian faith regarding helping the poor or converting social systems from bias to deep fairness escape directives or laws imposed from outside. Because they flow from the visions of our neighbors that come in times of grace—visions that reveal our neighbors to be the prime places where God asks our help—our most creative efforts to promote social justice are intimate, concrete, proportioned to given circumstances in ways that no general decrees can be.

The main function of church regulations and theologians' advice, it follows, is to give our prayer and social service general guidelines. At their best, such guidelines make available the wisdom of a long and rich tradition. For example, they remind us that prayer that makes us eccentric or proud or isolated from the community is suspect. For another example, they remind us that God loves all human beings, and so that no analysis of social conflicts that nourishes antagonism between social classes comes from God. The more experienced we become at either prayer or work for social justice, the more we appreciate the wisdom of those who have preceded us in these endeavors. Both zones of a basic, fully adequate Christian spirituality invite considerable self-deception.

The history of prayer, and the history of movements for social reform, are replete with stories of people who began well but eventually wandered far afield. So to grant spirituality some independence of outside controls and insist that its first authority is the Holy Spirit is not to despise or disparage what those who know the Christian tradition have to offer. Only fools would neglect the witness of the past, or the teaching of present church authorities. As always, the sign of a healthy spirituality is its balance—its lovely poise between craven submission and reckless independence.

What a healthy spirituality both seeks and enjoys is a full measure of inner freedom. Liberated from both oppressive external powers and equally oppressive internal voices (of pride, fear, self-importance), a healthy spirituality is equally able to say yes or no. If the Spirit of God fills decrees of church officials with wisdom, they become the manifest will of God. If theologians' interpretations of tradition seem wise in suggesting constraints on present experiments, then constrained such experiments will be. And even the trickiest portion of such spiritual discernment, determining whether one is in fact free enough to interpret where wisdom and the will of God lie, tends to work out well enough, over time, when people keep praying, sharing their convictions, and putting their faith on the line for social justice. Our potential for self-deception may only cease at the grave, but Catholic theology is hopeful enough about human nature and divine grace to ensure that this potential need not cripple our spiritual venturing.

It remains to be said that, for our topic of what Catholic spirituality may learn from the history of religions, the Catholic view of both human nature and divine grace does encourage hopefulness. As Christians approach the testimony of Hindu yogins, Buddhist monks, Muslim sufis, Jewish rabbis, and others who tell wonderful stories about religious experience, they need not fear diabolical error. The God who has not left divinity without witness anywhere ensures that every bit of healthy, attractive humanity testifies to the divine presence. Wherever people are honest, good, faithful, loving, self-sacrificing, reverent toward the mystery of creation, and the other virtuous things we find moving us to admiration, the Spirit of God has to be working in their depths. There is no humanity apart from divine grace, and this in two senses. First, no human being falls outside God's providential care and plan of salvation. Second, every time that a person makes human existence admirable, this care and plan come into perceptible focus. So Paul told the Philippians, "whatever is true, whatever is honorable, whatever is just, whatever is pure, whatever is lovely, whatever is gracious, if there is any excellence, if there is anything worthy of praise, think about these things" (4:8).

Christians need not fear the cultures of non-Christians, especially their religious achievements. God is the Lord of all history and culture. And it makes sense to believe that all peoples can be tutors to one another—witnesses to what wit and grace can accomplish. Some of the most important witnesses tell us how to endure sufferings, even evils. Others tell us how to open ourselves to peak experiences, where divine beauty may enrapture our hearts. The witnesses that bear on self-knowledge are extremely precious. The witnesses that shore up our hopes that love is stronger than death have clearly come from God, the deathless one.

So we may regard the history of religions as a great school for our instruction. What we can learn from eminent, and even ordinary, people of other faiths is another font of revelation, alongside scripture, Christian tradition, and the workings of God in the natural world. Certainly we have to separate the wheat from the chaff. Naturally we have to test the spirits and see whether a given teaching or practice from an outside tradition squares with our legacy from Christ. But in an important way we can begin to reject the distinction between "outside" and "inside," because we can begin to realize that all people hold in common the two most important determinants of culture and religion: human nature and the grace of God. That is the most catholic assumption we can make, and so the one we make foundational for this venture in Catholic spirituality.

Prayer and Social Justice

A viable spirituality deals with all important aspects of people's lives. Their minds, their bodies, their affections, their work, their play, their worship, their ways of coping with sickness and death—all is grist for its mill. So it is only to simplify matters that we concentrate on prayer and social justice. True, this concentration bears a helpful resemblance to the twofold commandment summarizing Jesus' religious program: love of God with whole mind, heart, soul, and strength, and love of neighbor as self. Still, we are not implying that prayer is the only way to love God, or that work for social justice is not obedience to God's will. Equally, we are not implying that prayer cannot be a profound love of neighbor as oneself, or that social justice is the only debt we owe our neighbors. Finally, we should say that "social justice" ought to include work to safeguard the natural environment, and that many species of prayer celebrate the goodness of creation. Ideally, therefore, our twofold concentration will merely epitomize a spirituality that covers all four of the primordial dimensions of human existence: nature, society, the self, and divinity. Ideally, what we appropriate from outside sources will stimulate a richer flourishing of all the main preoccupations of a healthy Catholic spirituality.

Why is it that prayer so frequently occupies center stage in impressive spiritualities? Because prayer is the best name we have for direct contact with, experience of, God. God is the crux of human existence, as religious people see it. Thus our attempts to deal with God have to stand among the most important concerns of our lives. For Christian faith, the coin in which God deals is love. Of all the signs, the hints, that we have about the nature of God, love is the most privileged. The love that Christian faith finds so important to discerning the presence and nature of God is a mixture of desire (*eros*), self-sacrificing benevolence (*agape*), and friendship (*philia*). It compounds our deepest need and our most ecstatic emotion. The best in us, the best that happens to us, reveals the full transcendence of God—how God our creator and redeemer, our parent and lover, must be. The worst in us, our torpor and sin, reveals how completely we need a transcendent God.

Only if God is good beyond our human capacity can we hope to enter upon an existence corresponding to our hearts' most ardent longing. Human beings cannot save themselves. For Christian faith, the wonder of divine grace is that God fashioned a way to make human nature God's own intimate concern, assuming flesh and defeating both sin and death. Thus Christian prayer does not blush to praise God ceaselessly, ask God night and day for daily bread (all that God's people need), and insist that God wants a fully incarnate response—sights, sounds, gestures; words and sacraments; song and dance. Prayer therefore stretches out to include everything intimate and powerful in Christian life. Just as faith sees all good gifts descending from a Father of lights above, so it sees all decent human concerns and achievements ascending to God, as return of the gifts that God has bestowed.

If much of prayer passes along a vertical axis, orienting earthly creatures to the heavenly abode of their God, much of social action passes along a horizontal axis, between neighbors. Certainly, there are moments of prayer, dimensions of prayer, that bring out the immanence of God. God is more intimate to us than we are to ourselves, so many of the saints have gone within to find the Spirit of God, or the divine child gestating in their spirits. Certainly there are moments when work for social justice cracks open the presence of heaven within time, of utopia within causes thought limited to given places and goals. The same human spirit that makes our prayer lively, that causes each day to stretch out as another claim upon God for bread and forgiveness, makes our struggles for social justice, whether great or small, three-dimensional.

There is no honest politics, or education, or social service, or art, or science, or parenting that cannot become a sacrament, a communiqué of God's love and care. There is no good meeting between people, whether they be lovers, friends, co-workers, or even enemies, that cannot become space rendered pregnant with divine meaning, a womb for human growth. When people truly meet one another, in contrast to their normal passing by, their resonance tells of the divine Spirit. Two or three people gathered together for important work, work in which they have invested themselves, regularly feel the touch of God. Even when their work seems to go badly, so that their communion falters, faith can find a presence of God—at the least, the peculiar presence that is the divine absence (awkwardness, pain, the lack of grace).

The divinity at the center of every significant spirituality, because at the center of every adequate understanding of human nature, deals in paradoxes such as presence-through-absence. If we fly to the highest heavens of ecstasy, God is there. If we fall to the depths of alienation and depravity, God is there, burning in our pain. God has so tilted the game that we cannot enjoy our depravity. Even in ruining ourselves, we learn that God has made us for holiness—love strong enough to make us transparent, so that we need not blush. We could not sin if we were not free to act better. We could not despair if we had never hoped. It isn't fair, this way that God has arranged human existence. It gives our rebellion, our fear, and all the other ways that the disproportion between us and God expresses itself no parity with our chances for saying yes to God. God loves us so intrinsically that both our pleasure and our pain take us to divinity. We are so completely made for God that both success and failure, both virtue and vice, involve us in divine providence. To serve God is to reign as free and sovereign. To rebel against God is to enter upon a slavery from which only God can liberate us. Sometimes this comes home so forcefully to people who pray that they have to laugh. Like the prodigal son, slumping home in well-won disgrace, people who pray find that God doesn't care about their failures, because God is so delighted to have them back.

Perhaps the most effective work for social justice replicates this pattern of free forgiveness and restitution to the bosom of God's family. When people forgive their enemies, offering a new start, the divine judgment that all offspring are precious in their simple being can take hold. It is not what people have done, evil or good, that keeps them dear to God (and so dear to those being educated in God's values). It is what people are, what people remain until their last breath (and, for faith, beyond death, into eternity). People are offspring of God, images of the image of God that took flesh in Jesus of Nazareth. That is how Christian faith struggles to see all human beings, whether friends or foes. When any of us was a sinner, God loved us. As long as any of us wishes, the love of God can take over our hearts and transform our lives.

People who work to cure the sick, enlighten the ignorant, house the homeless, feed the hungry, and, most generally, love the unloved—such people make "social justice" a conduit of salvation. Even when they are not aware of the theological implications of their work, or would blush to account their work an extension of Christ's ministry, their work itself extends what God's emissary came into the world to accomplish. And since God's emissary was the Word in whom all things in creation hold together (Col 1:17), any work for social justice, like any prayer, flows through his centrality. Buddhist works of charity, Muslim almsgiving, Jewish concern for human rights, Hindu fidelity to *dharma* —all strike the Christian as manifestations of the righteousness of the cosmic Christ. There is nothing decent in human existence that is foreign to this Christ. There is no suffering or triumph that cannot be illumined by his cross and resurrection. So Christian spirituality has to grant God a blank check. All prayer that magnifies the divine name and repents of sin enters into the divine liturgy, where the Spirit and the risen Lord celebrate the Father. All social justice carries into the world and back to God the circulation of the three divine persons, whose life is pure light and love. In the ultimate perspective that most encourages passionate Christians, divinity itself is the prime mover in all human endeavors, ensuring that none is meaningless or cannot be redeemed.

This Book

Having considered what we mean by "the history of religions" and "Catholic spirituality," and explained how we expect our focus on prayer and social justice to function, let us conclude this Introduction by describing the contents of the rest of this volume. In the next chapter we deal with religions of oral peoples. "Oral peoples" include prehistoric peoples, who lived before the rise of writing less than six thousand years ago, and peoples who remained non-literate for some part of the historical era. The most interesting aspect of oral religious cultures, for our purposes, is the immediacy that oral traditioning creates.

Without written texts, people tend to deal with their myths and rituals intimately, allowing them to have a great impact. Characteristically, dreams and other forms of psychic suggestion mix in with disciplined observation and speculation, creating what some scholars call an "undifferentiated" consciousness.[2] Oral peoples tend to be deeply sensitive to the rhythms of nature, for nature is their first font of revelation. Their divinities speak to their humanity, but often through storms or encounters with animals. We reflect on some of the wisdom that prehistoric peoples, native Americans, Africans, and Australians have accumulated through the centuries, asking what Catholic spirituality ought to make of this treasury. When Christians pray or work to make the world fit to live in, what might the experience of oral peoples offer them? What, in turn, might Christians offer oral peoples to clarify their best intuitions?

Our third and fourth chapters take up Asian traditions: Hinduism, Buddhism, Confucianism, Taoism, and Shinto. Obviously, our polling of these traditions, like our polling of oral traditions, can only be very limited. Nonetheless, it may profit our reflections about the requirements for a viable Christian spirituality to engage with Asian experiences of prayer (meditation) and social justice. All five of the traditions that we consider have long and rich histories. All five have been pathways through which millions of people have found deep meaning and beauty. Indeed, so many people have survived through recourse to Hindu, Buddhist, Confucian, Taoist, and Shinto beliefs and practices that any Christian spirituality wanting to be catholic has to take these traditions seriously. In our view, it has to take them sympathetically, as though receiving teachers who might illumine Christians' own struggles, if only because God obviously has given them many graces.

Chapter 5 deals with Judaism and Islam, sister religions to Christianity. Both Christianity and Islam owe a great deal to Judaism. One has only to open the Christian Bible and the Qur'an for that to be clear. All three faiths claim to be monotheistic, deriving from Abraham, Moses, and the other great prophetic figures who rule the Hebrew Bible. All three claim to offer salvation—healing from sin and amnesia. Yet the history of the relations among these three faiths is troubled, and the end of their troubles is not yet in sight. When any of the three becomes fundamentalist, the other two tend to suffer suspicion and antagonism, if not outright hatred. Nonetheless, Judaism and Islam have developed impressive schools of prayer, and impressive views and practices of social justice. In irenic perspective, both have much to teach docile Christians. A Catholic spirituality wanting to operate maturely in today's global culture does itself no favors by ignoring such potential enrichment. Certainly all Christians have to subject Jewish and Muslim spiritualities to the criterion of Jesus Christ, just as all Christians have to subject Asian and oral religions to the example and teaching of Jesus. But such "subjection" can be benign, because Christians can approach Jews and Muslims as wise teachers about the ways of divine grace.

In Chapter 6 we take up methodological issues, which tend to interest historians of religion. Such questions as the influence of faith, of non-faith, and of preconceptions about the nature of religion come in for much scholarly discussion. So does the question of sameness and difference across the religious traditions, the question of how a western category such as "divinity" relates to eastern equivalents (sometimes summarized by scholars as "ultimate reality"), and the question of how sacredness or holiness functions in oral traditions (in comparison with or contrast to its functions in western history). Historians of religion are interested in how historical studies ought to proceed, but also in how to generate categories for comparing religious traditions, how to read religious texts, and how the cultures with which a given religious tradition interacts tend to impinge on it. For our purposes, these methodological issues are especially interesting when they assume, or suggest, or impose restrictions on the primacy of Christian commitments. By reflecting on typical views of important historians of religion, we can better appreciate the foundational and methodological issues that Christian spirituality has to negotiate if it wants to appropriate the wisdom of other religious pathways.

Chapter 7, our Conclusion, offers us a final opportunity to reflect on the challenges that non-Christian views of prayer and social justice present. It also offers us an opportunity to reflect on the universal presence of the divine grace that Christians find best revealed in Jesus Christ, and on the divinity that has not left itself without witness anywhere. So our Conclusion takes us back to our beginning, but (we hope) sufficiently enriched by the intervening studies to make that beginning seem more intriguing. In fact, we are always making a new beginning at the task of appreciating God's work in the world. The divine beauty is ever new, as well as ever ancient. So any conclusion is at best provisional, bound to be supplanted when the urge arises once again to open our hearts to God's voice. As Hebrews puts it: "Today, when you hear his voice, do not harden your hearts as in the rebellion, on the day of testing, when your fathers put me to the test and saw my works for forty years" (3:7; see also 3:15, 4:7, and Ps 95:7–11).

In the "today" that all vital spiritualities stress, we may become contemporaries with those who faced the test in the past. What is the test? To keep faith, regardless of how daunting the apparent circumstances or foes. Nowadays, many Christians find the power and influence of other religious traditions, to say nothing of secular traditions, very daunting. Uncertain how to correlate them with a commitment to Christ, they can flee the test of letting God slowly reveal what is compatible and what is not. Apart from the specific yield of our reflections on the findings of the history of religions, we hope that our method and style in this book will also be helpful.

Our method is to approach outsiders confident that their best creations will remind us of the Christian God. Our style is to establish a conversation with representative outsiders—a take and give that assumes good will and proceeds to the infra-Christian task of estimating the implications of non-Christian experience and wisdom for Christian prayer and social justice. We want this proceeding to be natural, unself-conscious, unashamed of the instinct that moves it—the conviction that unless Christians bring what pleases or disturbs them to their God, the Christ who is the love of their lives, their spirituality will remain immature. Paul said that nothing can separate us from the love of God in Christ Jesus (Rom 8:39). We take Paul at his word, and so we anticipate only good things from this encounter with the history of religions.

NOTES

1. See, for example, John Hick and Paul Knitter, eds., THE MYTH OF CHRISTIAN UNIQUENESS (Maryknoll: Orbis, 1987); Leonard Swidler, ed., TOWARD A UNIVERSAL THEOLOGY OF RELIGION (Maryknoll: Orbis, 1987); Wilfred Cantwell Smith, TOWARDS A WORLD THEOLOGY (Philadelphia: Westminster, 1981); and also the first volume of this series, CHRISTIAN UNIQUENESS AND CATHOLIC SPIRITUALITY (New York: Paulist, 1990).

2. See our INTERPRETING THE RELIGIOUS EXPERIENCE (Englewood Cliffs: Prentice-Hall, 1987), which applies to the world religions Eric Voegelin's views of how consciousness has differentiated throughout history.

Chapter 2

Religions of Oral Peoples

Paleolithic Myths

Mircea Eliade, without doubt the most influential figure in the growth of the history of religions to academic and popular influence, has written of paleolithic peoples: "In short, it seems plausible to state that a certain number of myths were familiar to Paleolithic populations, first of all the cosmogonic myths and the myths of origin (origin of man, of game, of death, etc.). To give only one example, a cosmogonic myth brings on the stage the primordial Waters and the Creator, the latter either as anthropomorphic or in the form of an aquatic animal, descending to the bottom of the ocean to bring back the material necessary for the creation of the world. The immense dissemination of this cosmogony and its archaic structure point to a tradition inherited from earliest prehistory. Similarly, myths, legends, and rites related to ascent to the sky and 'magical flight' (wings, feathers of birds of prey—eagle, falcon) are universally documented, on all the continents, from Australia and South America to the Arctic. Now these myths are bound up with certain oneiric [dream] and ecstatic experiences specifically characteristic of shamanism, and their archaism is indubitable."[1]

The contention at work in this paragraph is that motifs that one can find in the cultures of recent oral peoples, when widespread and apparently stretching back into earliest memory, probably existed among Paleolithic peoples—the hunters and gatherers who dominated humanity during its first tens of thousands of years of existence and fashioned its earliest worldviews. Here Eliade singles out two preoccupations. The first is with the origins of the world. The second is with ascent to the sky and magical flight. The apparently prehistoric interest in the origins of the world assumes that the world is a living thing, and

so must have been born, or come into being in some way analogous to
the creation of animals and human beings that fascinated the earliest
peoples. At the creation of the world, things assumed the shape they
now have, so the creation of the world constituted the present world
order. When they recited their stories about the creation of the world,
oral peoples probably felt themselves drawn into the holiness of that
process itself. Certainly anthropologists and historians of religions who
have worked with recent oral peoples have found that their major rituals regularly included a repetition of their cosmogonic myths. At the
erection of a house, or the beginning of the new year, or the consecra-
tion of new adults, the desire to make a new start would prompt oral
peoples to renew their appreciation of the master-story giving all of
existence its structure. Thus, the cosmogonic myth tended to function
therapeutically. Not only did it allow oral peoples to think that the
world had sense and order, it also allowed them to make new starts and
so escape from the negativities of the old year, or the old phase of the
life cycle, or the old dwelling.

The motifs of ascent and magical flight that Eliade finds distrib-
uted throughout shamanic cultures reveal an equally touching desire.
The shaman tends to be the most important person in oral cultures,
because the shaman is the one who can escape from present, profane
existence and fly to the gods (the realm of stable, holy existence).
Whether the shaman does this to solve a problem (such as a mortal
sickness or a lack of game), or to guide the souls of the dead to the place
of rest, or simply to consort with the forces that alone are fully real, the
magical flight reveals the potential of human nature to transcend itself.
Human beings have a bodily part, which is indebted to matter and its
restrictions, but they also have a spiritual part, which can travel in
dreams, thought, and the ecstatic transports that shamans induce by
singing, drumming, dancing, fasting, and the other techniques passed
down by their kind through the centuries. This spiritual part of the
human being gives it some leverage against the passage of time and the
constraints of space. It opens a wide realm of creativity, where human
beings can explore and exploit what might have been, or what may still
come to pass. The "flight" associated with such familiar or helping
animals as eagles and falcons dramatizes this capacity of the human
being. Just as fierce, beautiful birds can escape the constraints of the
earth, so the human spirit can break its material bonds and soar to the
heavens—the realm of creativity, newness, and salvation.

When Christian theologians consider the implications of pre-historic stories about creation and shamanic symbols of transcendence, they profit most by assuming that prehistoric peoples were as human as themselves, that God had saving purposes for the most inspired prehistoric narratives and artworks, and that the place of Christ in the order of the universe and the ascent of the human spirit to God only becomes more impressive when one adds the testimony of prehistoric peoples to the argument that human beings by nature seek ultimate explanations and escape from mortality to the deathlessness of God.

Thus, without worrying about the particulars of a given cosmogony, Christian theologians can rejoice in the effort of earliest human beings to endow their world with pattern, order, and meaning. Realizing that the world does not explain itself, paleolithic peoples worked out stories of how outside forces might have formed the earth to its present shape. Equally they worked out stories to explain the appearance, powers, and condition of humanity, the animal world, the world of plants, and the world of inanimate things. Always the parents of such mythology were the twin urges to understand the world in which human beings had been placed and to safeguard humankind from the threats in that world. Shamanic voyages sprang from much the same motivation. By searching for cures, signs of meaning, experiences of harmony with sacral powers, and the like, shamans argued implicitly that salvation had to be possible. To paraphrase Pascal, they would not have searched so diligently had they not been found, seized, by the conviction that health, meaning, and even immortality constitute the rightful human condition.

When people move into their myths, so that they live among the core symbols, make themselves contemporaries with the characters in the leading stories, and sing or dance their way to union with the dramas that the myths unfold, they take a giant step toward the divine mystery. Their mythopoeia in fact is a form of prayer: a direct address of the divinity responsible for the human search for salvation. What strikes the present-day Christian interested in a spirituality responsive to the full range of human experience is the vitality of oral people's myths and rituals. Before the advent of a secular mentality that denied transcendence, humanity was convinced that the most important aspect of its life was its intercourse with the sacred—the really real that limited, cracked human existence could only glimpse occasionally.

One finds this conviction among the desert fathers of early Christianity, who lived in the hope of escaping the unreality of the world and finding in communion with God a truly stable, satisfying way of life.[2] The transports of the desert fathers in prayer (which they prepared for by stern asceticism quite like much shamanic discipline) are reminiscent of the journeys of shamans that apparently stretch back to archaic times. Certainly the desert fathers, reflecting on the Bible as the font of all useful knowledge, interpreted their religious transports as effects of efforts to love a God who is pure spirit and truth. They left the world of oral peoples, inasmuch as that world made nature the prime deity and focused little on a divinity that could not be imagined, could only be grasped in faith. Yet it is not certain that prehistoric peoples had no intuitions that ultimate reality lies beyond the human imagination, because to have such intuitions they need only have had ineffable experiences, or reflected on the gratuity of peak experiences, or pondered how no one, no matter how venerable, could grasp the reason for death or the state of those who had died. Even the best shamanic images and stories only seemed plausible in the heat of religious ceremony. Afterward, uncertainty and agnosticism could settle in. But agnosticism can be the threshold to a confession that we can never escape mystery. When it was that for prehistoric human beings, they were halfway to being anonymous Christians.

Paleolithic Justice

The second half of an anonymous Christianity concerns social justice. If the flight of the human spirit to God in prayer, mythic contemplation, religious ceremony, shamanic ecstasy, and the like expresses a core desire to deal with what is most real and valuable, efforts to make life on earth peaceful, just, beautiful, fertile, kindly, and the like express a core intuition that any righteous rebound from human spirituality builds solidarity and community. The evidence about prehistoric cultures seldom allows a full reconstruction of how the people lived and what they thought about justice, but archeological work has produced provocative data that suggest a peaceful culture in Old Europe, before the invasion of warlike Indo-Europeans.

Marija Gimbutas has published a thorough study of the images from Old Europe that archeologists have found, many of them suggesting the centrality of a goddess-figure representing the mysteries of birth and death. While her focus has been the period beginning with early agriculture in Europe, between eight and nine thousand years ago, she believes that the roots of symbolism about the goddess lie as far back as 25000 B.C. In contrast to the Kurgan culture that arose in southern Russia around 4500 B.C., the culture of Old Europe was peaceful and considered women at least the equals of men: "The Goddess-centered art, with its striking absence of images of warfare and male domination, reflects a social order in which women as heads of clans or queen-priestesses played a central part. Old Europe and Anatolia, as well as Minoan Crete, were a gylany [a social structure in which the sexes were equal]. A balanced, nonpatriarchal and nonmatriarchal social system is reflected by religion, mythologies, and folklore, by studies of the social structure of Old European and Minoan cultures, and is supported by the continuity of the elements of a matrilinear system in ancient Greece, Etruria, Rome, the Basque, and other countries of Europe."[3]

While this proposition may be conjectural, it remains stimulating. If the oldest remains from European archeological sites suggest that humanity was not always divided sexually or preoccupied with violence, then people on the lookout for hopeful scenarios, ways of being human that might avoid modern destructiveness, should take notice—all the more so if such sites also suggest a harmony with nature that avoided the modern attitudes responsible for our current ecological crisis. Naturally, the span between 25000 B.C. and 2000 A.D. is a huge one, psychologically and culturally as well as temporally. Naturally, there are good reasons from Christian faith to doubt that humanity ever achieved a utopia. But a generous study of archaic humanity might well reveal that, when life was considerably simpler, certain key issues may have stood forth more clearly and received better handling than they do nowadays.

For example, few things are more pertinent to social justice, closer to its daily residence or absence, than fair-dealing between the sexes. Social anthropologists and philosophers can debate whether the most crucial differences among human beings are racial, economic, or sexual, but by any tally the division into female and male seems primordial. From this division or differentiation comes life itself. So if life is to seem good and go well, on many different levels, men and women have to get along. If Old Europe did in fact create a gylany, then Old Europe has much to teach us. In our modern cultures the relations between the sexes have been so ambiguous that both women and men have suffered a great deal. Only fools would not admire something better.

Similarly, if Old European cultures managed to interact with nature—the earth, the plants, the animals—peaceably, neither destroying their habitats nor being destroyed by natural forces, then they accomplished something we moderns have yet to prove we can. Certainly, one can ask what standard of living Old Europeans achieved, how long they usually lived, whether their lives were rich or brutish. But if we are in a posture of learning, we will not make such questions a hindrance to learning how nature functioned in the Old European psyche and why Old Europeans survived through so many millennia.

In an evolutionary view of human history, one can assume that later peoples built on the achievements of earlier ones. An evolutionary view does not have to assume that everything later was better. We need not try to fit history to a pattern of constant progress. But nowadays we can self-consciously approach the past as a source of instruction. If the model of the golden age, according to which earliest humanity must have been wisest humanity, does not hold, neither does the model according to which prior ages must have been benighted. The best model, in our view, is one in which we consider human beings equal in their need to solve such fundamental problems as how to survive physically, how to create cultures that will make life seem good, how to cope spiritually with death, suffering, and evil, and how to reconcile themselves to the inevitable mysteriousness of the human condition. Whatever one people or culture creates that helps them cope well and hold their own against such fundamental problems should be grist for other peoples' mills.

Now, Christians (and other people who believe themselves to be the recipients of divine revelation) have special problems achieving this egalitarian frame of mind, but on their own terms they need not. To say that Christ is the incarnation of divine wisdom, the absolute redeemer, the perfection of humanity, and the like, as central Christian doctrine does, is not to say that the followers of Christ share fully in such achievements. Indeed, to say that Christ is all of these wonderful things is to suggest that everywhere, in all cultures, people have been beneficiaries of Christ, and that their best creations have hinted at the inexhaustible fullness of Christ.

For God, who exists outside of time, the Logos incarnate can easily be the pattern according to which all human beings create, develop, and grow. We human speculators will always have trouble with the eternity of God, perhaps especially when the before and after of history have become our guiding mentality, but that only reminds us that we are not God and should not presume to say how God looks upon world history. Christ, and so Christianity, will always have a priority in Christians' views of world history, but both the data of world history and the mysteriousness (the too-fullness) of divine providence can pry the hands of Christians away from making such a priority a stuffy certitude—something "dogmatic" in the pejorative sense. Christians can insist that Christ's twofold commandment is the consummate law, the norm for spirituality, ethics, and religious wisdom alike, without insisting that the goddess of Old Europe has nothing to teach them about what love of God and love of neighbor meant in the distant past and might mean again in the near future.

Reflections on the archeological finds from Old Europe send shivers down the spine because they remind us how long and mysterious the human story has been. If people were venerating the mysteries of life and death more than 25,000 years ago, then more than 25,000 years ago women and men, however different from us in appearance, were our spiritual kin. What did they learn, through their venerations? Was their world richer in revelations of the God who can still enflame our hearts, of the humanity that can still seem to us so lovable that it has to be stronger than death? Or were the hardships of their days the equivalents of what we suffer, so that, on balance, they had neither advantage nor disadvantage over us? Perhaps that would be the happiest hypothesis: the oldest Europeans, or early human beings generally, were like us in all things, including sin, and so would sympathize with our current struggles to forge viable, enspiriting cultures.

Native American Creation Accounts

In his remarkable study of South American religions, *Icanchu's Drum,* Lawrence E. Sullivan has underscored the search for meaning that permeates even the most apparently disorganized or bizarre mythologies. For our interests, this search suggests that, however different their thought-forms, oral peoples were pursuing the same sort of solutions and satisfactions that we Christians have pursued through theology and contemplative prayer. Indeed, just as early Christians could not separate theology and prayer, because they were seeking a knowledge of God that would transform their minds and hearts, so many oral peoples used their myths as means to contemplate the ultimate powers responsible for the world, asking their help or favor.

This seems to have been true regarding South American equivalents of the Christian belief about creation from nothingness: "A number of accounts describe the creation of the world from nothing (*creatio ex nihilo*). Supreme beings figure largely in cosmogonies that begin with an absolute and presymbolic state prior to any created condition. For instance, according to the Ona (Selknam) of Tierra del Fuego, the eternal supreme being, Temaukel, created the flat earth and the sky. The sky that he created was unmarked by the passage of time. It possessed neither stars nor planets. Similarly the earth was an undifferentiated space without mountains or rivers. The temporal markers of the sky and the spatial markers of the earth were formed later by the culture hero, Kenos. Kenos likewise created the animals and meteorological phenomena that filled the differentiated earth and sky."[4]

The absolute and presymbolic state may reflect the intuition of the human consciousness that something is prior to awareness. Human beings experience the rise of images and insights from what can seem to be a dark depth or priority—a kind of being that precedes awareness. Thus theories of consciousness developed by yogins (specialists in evacuating notice of particular images and thoughts) tend to depict various layers, the most basic of which lie below awareness. Inasmuch as awareness correlates with light, these basic levels of consciousness are dark. One can call them a being, an existence, that has yet to come to awareness, or a being that is more fundamental than awareness. "Fundamental" is an ambiguous term, suggesting that something more primordial may contain awareness, at least in germ, without spotlighting it. Thus theories of consciousness of a yogic sort can support the notion of a non-being equiprimordial with being—a darkness, or unconscious existence, partnered to, or perhaps even the parent of, light and conscious existence.

Whatever the source of given intuitions about the reality that existed prior to the creation of the material world that human beings know, it is instructive that this material world seldom seems to be its own explanation. Whether from psychic or other sources, human beings regularly believe that a reality ultimate enough to ground and explain the material world has to differ from it considerably. For example, it has to be stable, whereas the material world is mutable (as well as stable). It has to be absolute, free of dependencies and other sorts of conditions, for otherwise it would beg explanation as much as the material world does. Thus the originating deity of the Ona, Temaukel, was eternal. Standing outside of time, his works could be of a different order. The Ona apparently required a "heaven" (realm of Temaukel) on the order of the creation that they knew, so they had Temaukel create a sky different from the one that they knew, yet not absolutely so.

This points to the tendency of human beings everywhere to assume an analogy of being: the ultimate is, or does things, both like and unlike what human beings know. If the ultimate were completely different from human beings, human beings could have no contact with it, no portion in it, no help from it. On the other hand, if the ultimate were not significantly different from human beings, it would be of no use, for human beings require something of an other order—an order where change, finitude, death, and the other negative existentials that mark human existence down for suffering do not obtain.

We Christians sometimes forget the relation between prayer and the search for an ultimate whose being is only analogous to our own. Properly impressed by the personalism of God, and intent on the images of Christ the savior, we can fail to appreciate the thrust of all human spirits toward transcendence. The masters of Christian prayer have known better. While they have not neglected the images of the Logos incarnate, nor strayed far from scripture, they have had to report that many movements of the human spirit take it into the darkness of the divine otherness. There, in what the gospel of John (4:24) calls "spirit and truth," human beings learn that God is so simple and pure a mysterious fullness of being and love that much in their anticipation about God has to change, if they are to progress to full intimacy. Whether one calls the process by which human beings are transformed so that they can progress to full intimacy residence in a cloud of unknowing or suffering through a dark night of the soul, the point remains the same: to experience divinity directly is to die to spontaneous human assumptions. Divinity is different, as well as more intimate than we are to ourselves. Divinity is free of the conditions that shape so much of human existence.

Let us assume that the myths of native South Americans, and many other peoples, both express and mediate their experiences of ultimate reality. If we do, we find that much in the imaginative worlds that their myths create expresses (admittedly in different symbolism) convictions that Christian spiritual masters have explained in terms of finitude and sin. For the Christian masters, the human being can never comprehend God. God is without limit, infinite, while the human being is limited through and through. Granted, the human spirit possesses a certain infinity, inasmuch as it is never satisfied with its current state of either knowledge or love, and certainly this dissatisfaction keeps it searching for God, the one who might finally slake its thirst. But even in its spirituality the human being is limited, having no idea of the range of the divine spirituality and little part in a self-possession (the key mark of spirit) that is not intrinsically ordered to materiality.

Additionally the human being is marked through and through by sin: self-love to the exclusion of God, other people, and simple realism; disorder and disproportion that throw it, and those with whom it deals, out of joint. Indeed the masters of Christian prayer say that God must cleanse the human being of its sinful egocentricity, if it is ever to be fit for union with the divine. This cleansing is very painful, for it teaches the human being that apart from God it is nothing, either ontologically or morally. Where the sinfulness that seems to mark the human being from the earliest ages of its responsibility comes from is mysterious—as the symbol of "original sin" suggests. But the reality of such sinfulness preoccupies all the saints, because it is the source of their worst pains.

In contemplating the intuitions of oral peoples such as the South American Ona that original reality (divinity) is significantly different from anything in the material world, we need not grant them any exemptions from finitude and sinfulness. Perhaps Christian tradition has clarified both of these notions more than what has been typical of tribal South Americans, but those with eyes to see usually find that native traditions have been well aware that human being is limited as being itself need not be, and that human being is flawed—ignorant or twisted in ways that many people find painful and believe need not exist. For a Christian spirituality trying to develop global sympathies, affinities with all of the personal places where divinity has left witness of its ultimacy and desire to heal, such tribal awareness is very winning—a sign of radical brotherhood and sisterhood. Thus Christians wanting to expand their sense of the reality they meet in prayer can study native American traditions hopefully, anticipating significant instruction.

Meso-American Images

Among the most important documents that suggest how natives of Central America thought about the world prior to the advent of Christianity is the *Popul Vuh,* considered a compendium of traditional Mayan wisdom influenced by Christian notions but still faithful to pre-Christian beliefs. Notice the association between quiet and the existence of the creative powers prior to their making the earthly world: "Here is the description of these things: truly it was yet quiet, truly it was yet stilled. It was quiet. Truly it was calm. Truly it was solitary and it was also still empty, the womb of heaven. There are truly then the first words, the first utterances. There was not one person yet, one animal, deer, bird, fish, crab, tree, rock, hole, canyon, meadow or forest. All by itself the sky existed. The face of the earth was not yet visible. All by itself the sea lay dammed, and the womb of heaven, everything. There was nothing whatever silenced or at rest. Each thing was made silent, each thing was made calm, was made invisible, was made to rest in heaven. There was not, then, anything in fact that was standing there. Only the pooled water, only the flat sea. All by itself it lay dammed. There was not, then, anything in fact that might have existed. It was just still, it was quiet in the darkness, in the night. All alone the Former and Shaper, Majesty, and Quetzal Serpent, the Mothers and Fathers were in the water."[5]

Other parts of this creation account deal with the appearance of various features of the present earth. In the beginning, though, quiet, stillness, and darkness prevailed. Here the analogue may be the quiet of consciousness before illumination, clarifying focus on particular things to be known, but the more manifest analogue is gestation in the womb. In darkness, quiet, and hiddenness, the fetus assembles itself and prepares to come forth. The same with the gestation of the present world order in the cosmic womb. This account does not present creation as a making from nothingness. It is ambiguous about the status of the creative forces and the creatures to be brought forth, prior to the process of creation itself. Yet the main suggestion is that, whether we should consider them not yet formed or formed but held in stillness, the various creatures that we now know were secondary to a primordial quietude.

In the beginning, at the origins of being (rather than creation), the master-motif was a peace and darkness that we now only glimpse occasionally. It is not certain that the minds behind these texts would have agreed with Indo-European thinkers who considered self-possession, passivity, and peace more divine (or at least more characteristic of masculine deity) than self-dispersion through action and creative energy. But it is certain that, when they reached for symbols of the otherness from which the world they now knew had to have issued, they grasped figures prominent in physical or mental gestation: quiet, stillness, calm, darkness.

It would be imbalanced to suggest that contemplative experience the world over favors such passive or negative symbols, yet it would be inaccurate not to note the strength of such symbols. In fact oral peoples, and peoples who have left written records, both have experimented with numerous ways of contemplating ultimate reality. On the whole, existential, personally involving ways have been more significant than academic, detached ways. So, on the whole, people probably performed the contemplative exercises that apparently lie under texts such as the *Popul Vuh* (exercises with roots in oral, pretextual times) in the hope of encountering the forces that ran their world. By imagining the state of affairs described in the creation account, lingering with the images and taking them to be authentic, venerable reports of how things were (note the repetition of the assuring word "truly"), traditional Meso-Americans might become contemporaries of those events. With or without shamanic ecstasy, they might "travel" to the crucial time when the world arose, just as Christians have long "traveled" to Galilee and become contemporaries of Jesus walking on the water or transfigured before Peter, James, and John. The point to the journey is to arrive at the blessed event or scene that, one believes, reveals much about the significance or proper direction of one's present life. The point is to stop and contemplate, absorb, be reformed by the constitutive or paradigmatic primal happening.

The human spirit, ancient or contemporary, seems to assume that what happened in the beginning, or earlier in the causal chain, reveals a great deal about what came later, including what has come most recently, to establish present conditions. Yes, one can and should also ask questions about what comes at the end, as both ancient and contemporary people interested in wisdom do, but what began the process of creation or salvation retains a significant priority. What comes at the end lies in the future, at the term of whatever part of the cosmic passage stands between our "now" and the consummating "then." What occurred at the beginning seems more fixed, less obscure. Naturally, a critical approach to creation accounts notes that the "revelation" they claim makes them certain (and so establishes their fixity) owes a great deal to human imagination. Nonetheless the great impact that the early, parental phases of the evolutionary cycle make seems to bestow on them a singular authority.

On the whole, human beings have so strongly wanted or needed to believe in definite origins that they have blocked their awareness of the human component in the rise of "revealed" texts or truths and embraced canonical, "scriptural" accounts as uniquely privileged: the word of God or the gods. It does not matter that the evolutionary line that most oral and premodern peoples assumed was cyclical rather than linear. The primal, originating events still held pride of place, because they determined the structure of each rotation of the (sometimes endless) cycle of creation (and, sometimes, of destruction).

The import of these reflections for contemporary Catholic spirituality should include an awareness that the quiet and darkness prominent in this Meso-American account of creation (and in many others, including the creation in Genesis) have as deep roots in human experience as do the "noise" and "light" that come into play when the deities begin to make specific things. Everything that human beings regard as their scriptural or traditional authorities owes large debts to the human imagination. The differentiation of consciousness that Christians have good grounds for believing occurred with Jesus and in his wake sets such debts in a new light, but it does not remove them. Neither Christianity, nor Islam, nor Judaism enjoys a revelation dropped down from heaven or bypassing human consciousness (regardless of what fundamentalists in any of these traditions may say). The corrections of human instinct and imagination that encounters with divinity produce are still rendered in human terms—they must be, because we have no others. That is why the mystics and sages rightly considered closest to God and most trustworthy in their expositions of revelation so frequently assert that one cannot understand even the fraction of the divine mystery that human beings can understand unless one experiences God at first hand.

Without prayer, contemplative experience, moments when one's heart turns aglow with love, or when one is plunged into a dark night, one misses the full significance of a creation account, or a paradigmatic

story about exodus from slavery to freedom, or a report about resurrection and the sending of the Holy Spirit. There is no fully religious
reception of a scriptural text, no fully spiritual profiting from it, without taking it as *lectio divina*—material for personal rumination, material through which one may become contemporary with God and hear
the divine voice "today." This is not to say that Christian scripture is
merely allegory, or that it has no historical or literal or denotative
dimension. It is simply to say that, granted its historical, literal, and
denotative dimensions, it has been the word of God down the ages
because it has been considered, and experienced, to be much more.

For oral peoples, authoritative stories about the origins of the
world tended to come alive through ritual recitation. For Christians, it
has been much the same: scripture has been most vital at the divine
liturgy, where the community remembered its way to contemporaneity
with Christ and entered into the divine action being reported. Certainly, there were powerful analogues in private prayer, and few of the
saints experienced any division between the God they met at the liturgy
and the God they met in the solitude of their cells. But just as the
Meso-Americans who entered into the creation accounts of the *Popul
Vuh* strengthened their communal bonds by submitting themselves to a
common revelation of how the world had begun, so the Christians who
entered into the narratives about Jesus (the creator of their hopes for
salvation) strengthened their communal bonds by their common submission and knew thereby why their faith always assumed the church,
the fellowship of believers, to be its context and matrix.

A Sioux Vision

The equivalent of the church among many oral peoples is the
tribal community, yes, but also the entire fellowship of living creatures.
What nowadays commentators tend to call the "ecological" awareness
of native Americans and other oral peoples was not our present, self-
conscious effort to deal with the environment harmoniously but a spontaneous conviction that any encounter with ultimate reality moved
people to a deeper appreciation of their ties to everything that ultimate
reality embraced. One senses this in the report of Lame Deer, a Sioux
"medicine man," describing the vision that carried him from youth to
adulthood, and gave him his vocation. Lame Deer has fasted in solitude

for several days, and then experienced something birdlike hovering over him. Terrified, he has cried out for help. At the climax of his visionary experience a quasi-human voice reassures him: "I heard a human voice, too, strange and high-pitched, a voice which could not come from an ordinary, living being. All at once I was way up there with the birds. The hill with the vision pit was way above everything. I could look down even on the stars, and the moon was close to my left side. It seemed as though the earth and the stars were moving below me. A voice said, 'You are sacrificing yourself here to be a medicine man. In time you will be one. You will teach other medicine men. We are the fowl people, the winged ones, the eagles and the owls. We are a nation and you shall be our brother. You will never kill or harm any one of us. You are going to understand us whenever you come to seek a vision here on this hill. You will learn about herbs and roots, and you will heal people. You will ask them for nothing in return. A man's life is short. Make yours a worthy one.' "[6]

The shamanic imagery should be clear from our earlier use of Eliade's reflections: birds tend to represent spiritual flight, reaches of the human spirit toward a wisdom or fullness of reality (sacrality) associated with heaven. The social component in Lame Deer's vision is twofold. On the one hand, he will never injure the winged nation, because they are so closely associated with this formative experience. On the other hand, he will spend his life curing other human beings, for the sake of which he will learn about herbs and roots. Lame Deer's culture depended on a keen knowledge of the natural environment for both its medicines and its food and clothing. No supermarkets or pharmacies furnished the Sioux their necessities. The vision that commissioned Lame Deer therefore placed him right at the juncture between the natural and human worlds. His service of his fellow Sioux would depend upon his sensitivity to the earth, as well as to the sky. He had to learn about the sources of help (the gifts of divinity) available in the dirt, at the fundament of human existence, as well as about the forces associated with the heavens (and spiritual travel).

This has to strike the sensitive Christian as a wonderful incarnationalism. If ever one wanted a spirituality poised at the paradoxical center of human being, where men and women discover themselves to be deeply indebted to the earth yet always aspiring toward heaven, Lame Deer and his like provide it. At the present juncture, however, let us reflect on the "social justice" implicit in this vision and commission.

Human existence is short. Lame Dame will be wise if he makes his life significant by serving his fellow creatures. To become a healer, a medicine man, he will have to embark upon a significant discipline. But the motivation that can sustain him in his passage will be the awareness that he can make a difference to many people. Alleviating pain, spiritual as well as physical, he can serve the blessed powers who showed him such beauty and significance at his initiatory vision.

No doubt there are texts in which one can find native Americans debating how to establish a better justice, a sweeter peace, in their midst, but such do not leap from the pages of the anthologies. On the whole, oral peoples seem to assume that they know how they ought to live together, because their traditions make that plain. Their problem is finding and keeping bright the vision that would make social justice and peace concrete, practical. So, they have laid great stress on religious functionaries (shamans, medicine men, priests) who have worked to consort with the gods, to see visions and dream dreams. Such functionaries have furnished the entire tribe both practical help (healing, repair after the rupture of taboos, retention of traditional lore) and more basic psychic help: assurance that reality does have an intelligible structure and so can make sense. Because Lame Deer heard the speech of the bird people, he could assure his fellow Sioux, in all candor, that there were powers eager to help them make their way through the world and find rich meaning.

Christians who seek visions, experiences of God, could do far worse than to consider the medicinal career that Lame Deer sought. Whether one takes such a career narrowly (setting broken bones, fixing broken homes) or broadly (illumining darkened minds, shoring up battered spirits), the point remains the same. Most of humanity is suffering, groaning with pain. The more one learns about people's deeper, interior selves, the more one realizes that to be human is always to be in darkness and need. The few saints whom God grants steady experience of the divine love, usually after they have passed through formidable purification, are overbalanced by the great many people who are depressed, or hungry, or in sight of death. The meaning and healing that spiritual visions, contemplative experiences, bring to Christians, or any other people, are seldom given for the visionaries alone. The message, explicit or tacit, that they usually carry is that those who receive them ought to hand them on to their brothers and sisters. If God has loved us, we ought to love one another (1 Jn 4:11). If we have found healing, we ought to extend healing to others still suffering.

The political tasks that we assume simply by being citizens, members of various communities, people interdependent with men and women of many lands, boil down to forwarding the solidarity and healing that our gifts from God imply. Thus the Christian saints, raised high in prayer, have come back to earth renewed in their commitment to help the poor, comfort the suffering, enlighten those hunkering in darkness. The historians of religions tend to overlook the existential community that religious experiences of any significance spotlight. Regularly they miss the ties between a Lame Deer and the community of winged creatures who figured in his vision, because an academic mentality has little place for the energies of conversion. It can note their occurrence, but it is hard put to explain how they could take over a personality and change a life. On his own terms, Lame Deer emerged from his visionary quest both transformed and set on the pathway that he ended up traveling for the rest of his life. On Christian terms, he was blessed with a visitation of the Holy Spirit, the divine power committed to purifying him for deeper, more loving relations with both ultimate reality and his fellow creatures great and small.

Delaware Gratitude

On occasion Christians can come to a profound realization that only God can give them social justice. Such a realization stands forth in Martin Luther's grasp of justification by faith, and in Augustine's insights into the priority of divine grace. Perhaps the major reason why native Americans manifest little interest in political theory as such is that they too looked to divinity for the concord they sought. If they were to live together well, in prosperity and peace, they had to enjoy the enlightenment and strengthening of the Spirit responsible for their world. The cosmological tie is strong: divinity gives human beings all the things that they need to survive, so divinity is the one whom human beings ought continually to thank. The unspoken premise may well be that, if they are continually thanking divinity, human beings will enjoy good social relations (with non-human creatures as well as fellow men and women).

At the opening of an important Delaware religious festival, the Big House ceremony, the leader would customarily give a speech to set the tone for the days to come. One such speech began as follows: "We are thankful that so many of us are alive to meet together here once more, and that we are ready to hold our ceremonies in good faith. Now we shall meet here twelve nights in succession to pray to Our Creator, who has directed us to worship in this way. And these twelve *mesingw* [faces carved on posts] are here to watch and carry our prayers to Our Creator in the highest heaven. The reason why we dance at this time is to raise our prayers to him. Our attendants here, three women and three men, have the task of keeping everything about our House in good order, and of trying to keep peace, if there is trouble. They must haul wood and build fires, cook and sweep out the Big House. When they sweep, they must sweep both sides of the fire twelve times, which sweeps a road to heaven, just as they say that it takes twelve years to reach it."[7]

People gathering for such a ceremony affirm that they have come to revivify their common faith. They submit themselves to a common discipline, including the apportionment of roles and tasks. In the Delaware case, the focus of the twelve nights seems to be the creator, the source of all the good things that the tribe enjoys. Gathering to give thanks to the creator, to celebrate the divine bounty, brings joy to the people's hearts: "When we come into this house of ours we are glad, and thankful that we are well, and for everything that makes us feel good that the Creator has placed here for our use. We come here to pray him to have mercy on us for the year to come and to give us everything to make us happy; may we have good crops, and no dangerous storms, floods, or earthquakes. We all realize what he has put before us all through life, and that he has given us a way to pray to him and thank him."[8]

The prevailing mood is gratitude. Called to reflect on the year gone by and prepare for the year to come, the Delaware first call to mind all the benefits of the creator. Connected with this is a reaffirmation of their need. Without the creator's protection, they could find themselves defenseless against storms or earthquakes, against the failure of their crops or such other, unmentioned misfortunes as sickness. The marriage of gratitude for gifts received with petition for helps needed stands at the center of most peoples' prayer. When they come to themselves and realize their status as simply human beings, creatures whose lives are short and who cannot comprehend the divine mystery, they tend to raise their voices in both praise and request. In this passage, "prayer" seems to name petitioning the creator for help against misfortune. But the entire ceremony turns out to be a prayer, in the sense of a time when the people stand before their God and renew their inner life.

When Christians witness other people bowed low in prayer that could easily be their own, how should they react? What kinship may they draw from praise and petition like that of the Delaware? Clearly enough, they may draw a very close kinship—as close as their similarity in mortality, passibility, ignorance, and all the other expressions of human finitude that make human being itself a claim upon the divine mercy. Think about how God has made us all—men and women, old and great, whatever our color or tribe. Think about the fate we all share, simply because we belong to the same biological species. We all have to eat and drink, sleep and bestir ourselves. We all have to learn, to die, to fear sickness and other kinds of suffering. And we all have to wonder— at the beauty of the natural world, the indifference of the natural world, the power of human love, the twistedness of some human hearts, the overwhelming amount that we do not know, the gap between what we desire and what we obtain. Even the most blessed or content among us has to wonder about these things. In our wondering, our natural call to contemplation, we stand revealed as a species for whom prayer ought to be connatural.

One of the greatest benefits of studying people such as the Delaware is the realization that prayer was connatural for them. Regardless of their apportioning of tasks, and their dependence on special functionaries such as medicine men, they assumed that each man, woman, and child had a personal relation to the creator that demanded recognition. Each member of the tribe owed the creator thanks for the many good things previously bestowed and the many things needed in the year ahead. The wonder that the creator should have made provision in the past, and the hope that the creator would continue to make provision in the future, impinged on each Delaware person, because that wonder summed up where Delaware existence rooted.

Does Christian existence root in any different place? If Christians stand "in Christ," oriented toward the Father and supported by the Spirit, does this not merely color a dependence, an existential need, essentially the same as that of the Delaware? Certainly, if they wish, Christians can claim the history of Jesus, his revelations of the goodness of the Father and support of the Spirit, to make their prayer especially grateful. Certainly *eucharistia* can overwhelm petition. Yet petition remains not only valid but necessary. Jesus embraced petitionary prayer, making it central in his teaching about how to approach the Father. So the example of the Delaware in their Big House could buttress Christians in their churches, especially when it comes to the prayers of petition.

For interreligious dialogue, few things are more salutary, more encouraging, than discovering that, through our many different forms of prayer, we human beings of different religious traditions are usually preoccupied with the same tasks. We are praising the Father of lights, for good things received. We are petitioning our God for the help we need—especially for the communal agreement, the social peace, on which so much of our sense of life's goodness depends. When we are wise, we are also asking for peace with nature—the vision and strength to fit in with the ways that the creator has designed the world.

When they pray together for these basic human needs, to express these basic human instincts, people of different faiths weave bonds that no doctrinal differences can ever sever completely. Indeed, if their prayer goes well, bringing a mutual edification, partners to interreligious dialogue can position themselves for a more positive appreciation of one another's doctrinal views (ways of interpreting worship and work for social justice) than they are likely to do otherwise. The Delaware, preparing through their twelve day ceremony for their ultimate journey to heaven, offer us a wonderful reminder of the bottom line. The bottom line is that we are all under way to what we hope will be heaven, a zone where our thanksgiving will become a full-time occupation and our needs will fall away. The bottom line is our need for mutual support on this pilgrimage.

A Mashona Prayer

The prayers of the Mashona of Southern Rhodesia suggest that the concerns of many African tribes ran parallel with those of many native American tribes. Note in this hymn to Mwari, the Mashona Great Spirit, the accents of praise, petition, and wonder at the bounty of physical, natural life: "Great Spirit! Piler up of rocks into towering mountains! When thou stampest on the stone, the dust rises and fills the land. Hardness of the precipice; waters of the pool that turn into misty rain when stirred. Vessel overflowing with oil! Father of Runji, who seweth the heavens like cloth: let him knit together that which is below. Caller forth of the branching trees: thou bringest forth the shoots that they stand erect. Thou has filled the land with mankind. The dust rises on high, O Lord! Wonderful One, thou livest in the midst of the sheltering rocks. Thou givest of rain to mankind: we pray to thee, hear us, Lord! Show mercy when we beseech thee, Lord. Thou art on high with the spirits of the great. Thou raisest the grass-covered hills above the earth, and createst the rivers, Gracious One."[9]

The usual physical basis for the sense that God is spirit is the human experience of breath. Breath appears as a sign of full life: the infant draws its first breath, lets out a cry, and thenceforth seems fully human. Dying people complete their transition when they have ceased to breathe. Inasmuch as the natural world seems to be a living whole, it seems to depend on a source of breath—a quickening spirit. That quickening spirit is God, the source of life, the one who escapes mortality. Other analogies include human thought, which can move so swiftly, and the capacity of some part of the human makeup to travel in dreams or ecstatic states. The Great Spirit therefore is the one who is full of life, energy, movement, intelligence. The Great Spirit is the one on whom human beings pin their hopes, when they seek rest in their search for explanations of the natural world, or when they need the kind of help that nothing in the natural world, or in their own community, can provide.

When people conceive of a Great Spirit, a creator and stabilizer, they stand poised for worship. Inasmuch as the natural world solicits wonder and praise for its beauty and power, the natural world proclaims the grandeur of the Great Spirit. So the Mashona turn their awe at the towering mountains into praise of the Great Spirit ultimately responsible for those mountains (because ultimately responsible for everything that exists, animate or inanimate). The Great Spirit is powerful, and so fearsome, as well as awesome: consider what happens when the earth quakes and the mountains crumble. The Great Spirit must be the source of the heavenly pools that give rain, the fruits and grains that give oil, the forces that unify the heavens. May those forces, under the direction of the Great Spirit, create unity "below," on the earth that the heavens oversee, on the lower plane of existence where human beings dwell.

In a mood of worship, every beautiful or striking part of creation calls the Great Spirit to mind. The branching tree, and the process of growth through which it comes to stand tall, both bespeak the power and care of the Great Spirit. So do human beings, who fill the land and create problems. The dust rising to heaven symbolizes those problems —how human beings can trample nature down, how human error and need can create whirlwinds of pain. Far above all this, living on the heights and bestowing all that quickens life, the Great Spirit is the obvious one to petition in time of need.

The Mashona ask their Great Spirit, the Lord of their lives, to hear them. More, they ask their Great Spirit to be merciful—kindly, disposed to help—when they beseech heaven. Implied in this greater petition is an awareness of human failings. The world over human beings realize that they come before the creator, the ultimate recourse, with unclean hands and hearts. On the whole, human beings consider the deity to be holy, without the moral failings that they themselves display, so their approach to the deity is with fear and trembling. Even when they are filled with joy at the beauty that the Great Spirit has brought forth, or when they know that the Great Spirit must be surpassingly good, their own sense of imperfection gives them pause, may even fill them with dread. In asking God for what they need, many peoples make it clear that they have no right to be answered. Were God to deal with them according to strict justice, they could never be sure they would be heard. So they ask their deity to deal with them according to its better nature. They ask it to realize that human beings do not enjoy divine perfection or happiness, and to make this realization a source of pity (and so generosity).

The spirits of the great, who may be the heroes and heroines of yesteryear, the grandfathers and grandmothers of renown, enjoy the presence of the Great Spirit and, for this prayer, the Great Spirit enjoys their presence. Everything noble makes its way to the Great Spirit. At death human beings who have lived well can anticipate a complete fulfillment. The grass-covered hills, lovely, nutritious for cattle, and serene as troubled human beings hope to become after death, symbolize the capacity of the Great Spirit to make all manner of thing well. The rivers symbolize the flow of divine care, its moistening and slaking character. In a thousand ways, the heavens and the earth proclaim the glory of the Mashona Great Spirit. God is gracious—beautiful and bountiful—to the mind as well as to the eye, to the spirit as well as to the touch. Indeed, God is the gracious one—the source of all beauty and considerateness. Without God, the good things in the universe would have no foundation, and the Mashona would have nowhere to focus their hope.

The good things in the Christian's universe have their foundation in the Father to whom Jesus prayed regularly. The focus of Christian hope is what the Father made of Jesus—the maturation of his human-ity, so that at death it entered fully into God's own sort of existence. This "Father of Lights," as James (1:17) calls him, sends down from on high all the good things of creation. In another symbolism, not used by the New Testament but congruous with Christian faith, Christians could say that the divine is like mother earth, carrying a great bounty of life within, bringing forth good things from her depths. The point is the same one made by the Mashona: the splendors of creation tell of the divine splendor; the splendors of creation warrant our praising God and letting our awe rise toward heaven.

Can people of the twentieth century after Christ experience awe, when they have so dominated the natural world? Is not awe another of the primitive emotions that modern social studies have shown root in vulnerabilities that technology has overcome? Not if one listens to the pioneering scientists. Those exploring the galaxies, or trying to map our genetic endowment, or studying the intricacies of the sea, or investigat-ing the brain regularly speak as though they have been stunned by the complex beauty laid out before them. The natural world is far more impressive than what the traditions or prayers of the Mashona suggest. The power we should attribute to the Great Spirit behind the world, manifested in the world, stands on a different plane. But is there any reason to think that this so much more impressive power is also gracious, merciful, something or someone whom lowly, disfigured hu-man beings can petition? For Christians there is not only the human need for such graciousness, so persistent that if the Great Spirit were graceless the world would seem absurd, but also the person and teach-ing of Christ. The reason that Jesus could urge his hearers to love their enemies, do good, and lend without expecting anything in return was that the Most High "is kind to the ungrateful and the selfish" (Lk 6:35). The power that runs the world, that quickens all life, that heaps up the mountains and raises the grass-covered hills is gracious to the core. The mystery that flung the stars so far and causes the rain to fall is a parental love.

BaMbuti Solidarity

The BaMbuti of the Congo (Zaire) are pygmies who hunt and gather for their subsistence. The British anthropologist Colin Turnbull gave a stirring account of their lives in his celebrated book *The Forest People,* published in 1962. Among the many noteworthy anecdotes recorded in that book is the incident of Cephu, the bad hunter and reluctant member of the pygmy community. After distancing himself from the community (placing his lean-to at the edge of the communal circle, and refusing to participate in the regular ceremony of worship), Cephu went so far as to commit a grievous crime: "Ekianga leaped to his feet and brandished his hairy fist across the fire. He said that he hoped Cephu would fall on his spear and kill himself like the animal that he was. Who but an animal would steal meat from others? There were cries of rage from everyone, and Cephu burst into tears. Apparently, during the last cast of the nets Cephu, who had not trapped a single animal the whole day long, had slipped away from the others and set up his net in front of them. In this way he caught the first of the animals fleeing from the beaters, but he had not been able to retreat before he was discovered. I had never heard of this happening before, and it was obviously a serious offense. In a small and tightly knit hunting band, survival can be achieved only by the closest co-operation and by an elaborate system of reciprocal obligations which insures that everyone has some share in the day's catch. Some days one gets more than others, but nobody ever goes without. There is, as often as not, a great deal of squabbling over the division of the game, but that is expected, and nobody tries to take what is not his due."[10]

The sequel of this account is that Cephu is roundly criticized by the entire pygmy community, stripped of his ill-gotten gains, and forced to acknowledge his solidarity with the tribe. At the end Turnbull finds him participating in the common worship ceremony, apparently accepted back into the group with few second thoughts.

Consider the situation of hunters and gatherers such as the BaMbuti. For countless generations they have survived by their wits in the mighty Congo forest. The forest has become their beloved home, the god to whom they sing most nights. The forest seems to them extremely benevolent, providing all that they require for a decent existence. Yet they live from week to week, if not from day to day, and their survival depends on their cooperation. They have various ways of letting off steam, but when the chips are down they assume that all members of the group will cooperate for the common good.

In the background of Cephu's defection is some indication that he never felt fully part of the group that Turnbull was studying. In terms of kinship lines and blood affiliations, he was only a tangential member, more properly housed in another pygmy group. On the other hand, he lived with Turnbull's group, though on the fringes, and he benefited from their hunts and other projects. So while the group frowned on his separateness, gossiping against him, they assumed that, in the crunch, he would be one of them. When he showed that he was not, by violating a basic precept of the hunt, they turned on him angrily. It is interesting that no one struck him or threatened his life. It was enough to call him an animal, rather than a human being, and to cut him off from social contact. Immediately this brought him to his knees, and before long he was back in the tribal circle, apparently grateful to be readmitted to human intercourse. Apparently the threat of ostracism, and the common criticism of the group, were all the sanctions he needed.

When we talk about social justice, we moderns usually assume the context of the nation-state, or even of the international community now unifying around the globe. We live at considerable distance from the ancient human unit, the hunting tribe, and so we have lost the sense of solidarity that developed in their unit through tens of millennia. For ancient humanity, one could not be human apart from the tribe. Outside the tribe, the human group, there were only animals. People inside the tribe supported one another and made themselves trustworthy. If they did not, they were no better than animals. An animal was an outsider: at best an ally of the tribe, as a totem or a familiar; at worst an enemy, in combat with human beings for survival. Inasmuch as animals furnished hunters a significant part of their diet, animals were natural adversaries. To be called an animal, and accused of not being a human being, was a bitter fate—all the more so when one knew one had brought it on by one's own folly.

What manner of inner turmoil caused Cephu to violate so basic a precept as not stealing from others' nets is not clear. Neither Turnbull nor the pygmies go in for psychological reflection. Their focus is rather the common good of the tribe as a whole, to whom Cephu has become an irritant and a menace. Yet Cephu can get back to being tolerated, though not fully loved, simply by renouncing his eccentric ways and submitting again to the common disciplines. When he sits with the others for the nightly chorus of praise to the forest, he both affirms his solidarity with the rest of the tribe and asserts his right to membership in their human community.

Perhaps the pygmies have some doctrine according to which a tribe could continue to ostracize a deviant such as Cephu, but Turnbull's book gives no indication of that. More likely, the unwritten law is that, if a pygmy claims membership in the group and is willing to abide by its customs, he or she has to be admitted. No doubt the humiliation that Cephu suffered cut him more deeply than an outsider could appreciate, yet soon he was back in good graces, able to function again. This easy access to forgiveness and restoration is well worth pondering in a Christian context.

The Christian community, like the rest of the human community, is composed of many rag-tag, tatterdemalion members. Few are steadfast in sanctity or wisdom. Many fall flat on their faces, again and again. And yet the Spirit of God provides for all members, even the most difficult, by inspiring Jesus to encourage forgiveness again and again— seven times seventy (Mt 18:22) if necessary. The Christian sacrament of penance formalizes the processes of forgiveness, at its best making repentance heartfelt. Nonetheless, modern cultures have a difficult time with forgiveness and restoration to the bosom of the common community, as such conflicts as that between Protestants and Catholics in Northern Ireland, Jews and Arabs in Israel, and Muslims and Christians in Lebanon illustrate. None of the prophetic religions has been successful in inspiring a culture bent more on forgiveness and renewal than on justice or even vengeance. Each has to blush before the pygmies, who generally manage to limit their conflicts, and who allow deviant members easy readmittance to the community. In preferring social shame to physical violence, the pygmies give all the modern social groups an instructive lesson. If human beings were more threatened by ostracism from the tribe than by prison sentences or promises of physical punishment, we might see the revival of human solidarity.

The mystery of human togetherness, intuited by small groups such as the pygmies and symbolized grandly in figures such as Paul's "body of Christ," flickers and threatens to go out when people do not share a common way of life, do not depend on one another for survival. In fact we do continue to depend on one another for survival, as the current ecological crisis shows, but often we are too dim-witted to recognize how pollution of the waters or the air confirms our being members of one another and kin of the rest of natural creation. But Christians should stick to their own last and take to heart their own teachings about forgiveness. The hot alienation of Protestants and Catholics in Northern Ireland, and the cold alienations that continue to keep Protestant, Orthodox, and Catholics apart in the rest of the world, defying Jesus' teaching in John 17 and helping the world to reject Christ, are compelling evidence that many Christians remain utterly stupid about the gospel, utterly oblivious to the solidarity that divinity wants for all its children. Until the day when John 17 means more than Christians' private grievances, the churches will continue to be less human than the pygmies of the Congo forest.

A Maori Myth

The Maori, a Polynesian people of New Zealand, can represent the tendency of oral peoples to place human origins in a special creative activity of the divinity. The creation account that we study also suggests the ancient association between a feminine mother earth and a masculine father sky. Finally, the frank sexuality of the Maori story of the creation of woman reminds us that many oral peoples dealt with sexuality less personally, more cosmologically, than we moderns have tended to do. The first impression that sexual differentiation made throughout the tens of thousands of years when human beings hunted and gathered for their food was that this was the given means of physical renewal. For both animals and human beings, the survival of the species depended on the union of two complementary bodies. Feminists rightly question the extrapolation of such complementarity into a full-blown theory of masculinity and femininity, since throughout recorded history such extrapolations have tended to subordinate women to men, but at the elementary level where the interest of oral peoples focused, complementarity was the great force begging understanding.

Naturally, the development of what we now call personalist values, which make heterosexuality much more than simply a mechanism for reproduction, has to strike the Christian as great progress. Inasmuch as Christianity heralds the good news that God is love, the attraction between the sexes is bound to offer key analogies to the interactions between divinity and humanity. Still, it remains profitable to contemplate an earlier outlook such as that of the Maori, if only to heighten a Christian suspicion that God prepared the way for the revelation of divine love through millennia that schooled men and women in a mutual need, a common necessity that they cooperate to keep the tribe going.

"Tane [the Fertilizer] proceeded to the *puke* (*mons veneris*) of Papa (the Earth) and there fashioned in human form a figure in the earth. His next task was to endow that figure with life, with human life, life as known to human beings, and it is worthy of note that, in the account of this act, he is spoken of as Tane te waiora. It was the sunlight fertilizing the Earth Mother. Implanted in the lifeless image were the *wairua* (spirit) and *manawa ora* (breath of life), obtained from Io, the Supreme Being. The breath of Tane was directed upon the image, and the warmth affected it. The figure absorbed life, a faint life sigh was heard, the spirit manifested itself, and Hine-ahu-one, the Earth Formed Maid, sneezed, opened her eyes, and rose—a woman. Such was the Origin of Woman, formed from the substance of the Earth Mother, but animated by the divine Spirit that emanated from the Supreme Being, Io the great, Io of the Hidden Face, Io the Parent, and Io the Parentless."[11]

If we begin at the conclusion, we note the passion that comes over the old man who rendered this version of the Maori tradition about the creation of woman, when he contemplates Io, the Supreme Being. Tane and Papa, the fertilizing sky and the fertilized earth, are intermediary forces, gaining their power from Io. Io is the sole source of divine Spirit—animation, life, that depends on no other, that is intrinsic. Indeed, one suspects that the Supreme Being is supreme precisely because it is the sole source of animating spirit (though the account suggests that Io is more than simply spirit). Io is the great because, compared to Io, all other beings are small—penultimate at best. Io has a hidden face: no one has ever seen ultimate divinity. (To "see" God's face is a metaphor for understanding the mystery of existence. No human being has ever done this. To be human is to live in the midst of a creation, an existence, that one is constitutionally incapable of understanding. Historians of religion such as Mircea Eliade, who understand this basic fact of the human condition and orient their view of religion by it, tend to develop analyses of myths, rituals, and other key features of millennial human culture that stress wonder at life and death, sacrality and profanity. Historians of religion who do not stress the constitutional incapacity of humanity to understand its situation tend to produce analyses that, in our opinion, are superficial and denature what most religious groups have been struggling to accomplish.)

Though hidden from sight, Io is the parent of all creatures. In this account, the first woman arose because of the breath and warmth that Tane possessed from Io. The assumption probably is that Papa owes Io similar debts. As "parent," Io is androgynous, regardless of the imagery that other myths use to portray the divine action. The analogue in Christian theology is the "androgyny" of the Father, who has also to contain in himself the fertility associated with femininity, if his paternity is not to be misleading. As the unbegotten source of all that exists, divine or human, the Father is that beyond which one cannot go in one's searches for understanding or being. When Augustine developed the figure of memory for the Father, impressed by the fathomless storehouse of human recollection, he was close to making the Father uterine—that in which all finds its origin, from which everything issues.

The insight of the Maori into the primordial character of Io makes Io parentless. Like the unbegotten Father of Christian theology, Io depends on no other, is offspring of no other. Both Io and the Father are fonts of being and intelligibility. Both stop the process of regression to a more basic cause, representing the sufficiency of the divine mystery. To say "God" (Io or Father) is to name (blankly, with little specificity) the reality that is comprehensive, the reality that escapes all dominion, mental or physical, and gives all other realities their context.

To contemplate this reality is humanity's greatest satisfaction. Gazing on divinity with the eye of the spirit, loving its immensity and darkness from the heart or fine point of the soul, human beings have realized that only divinity could be their fulfillment. Somehow they had to become one with divinity. Somehow their love and intimate understanding had to tie them to Io or the Father with cords that could not unravel. In bolder imagery, they had to dissolve into divinity, or be raised to the right hand of the Father, or experience the spiritual presence of God as transforming them into deathlessness. The mystics who speak language such as this are unanimous that it fails badly. What they are trying to describe is so profound yet simple a transformation of the human condition that silence and warmth serve much better than nouns or verbs. The difference between knowing about divinity and being known by divinity to the core, like the difference between loving divinity and being loved by divinity to the core, is so dramatic, so chasmic, that all old languages fall away. In the figure of John of the Cross, gradually the flame takes over the life of the log, turning everything into its own fire.

Inasmuch as the first woman arose from the breath and light that Io gave Tare, the first woman may have been an offspring of the divine parent's love. All other women stand in the lineaments of the first woman, who herself rises on the pattern, from the sex, of Mother Earth. One could write a similar scenario for the origin of the first man, though here the correlation between masculinity and heaven might be a complicating factor. At any rate, the point in ancient mythologies is seldom to produce a logic of how humanity or the world at large arose. The point is usually to contemplate some striking features of the beings displayed coming into existence and intuit what they suggest about the ultimate, divine mystery holding all significance, all fates, in its grasp. In this myth the Maori gave themselves several good reasons to think that the first woman, emblem of beauty, fertility, pleasure, and the other boons stereotypically associated with femaleness in most oral cultures, arose from a process expressing the power and care of the Source of All. Thereby they gave themselves several good reasons to praise their divinity and magnify the divine name. Is not that what Christian accounts of creation, Christian reflections on femaleness and maleness, ought to do?

Australian Ambivalence about Sacred Forces

The aboriginal religions of Australia present diverse, rich mythic complexes, developed over thousands of years. One interesting feature of much aboriginal Australian mythology is the unethical behavior of numerous divine figures. Let us first present one description of this behavior and then reflect on its implications for primordial feelings about social justice.

Catherine Berndt, a well-established scholar of aboriginal Australian religions, has noted that "myths from all parts of the continent contain as much bad as good human behavior. The activities of a great many mythic characters do not conform with what was regarded as good behavior by, or for, the people who told and heard their stories. Even in regions where the main deities concentrate on creation in a relatively mild way, such as the Djanggawul (despite their original incest, and the men's theft of sacred paraphernalia), other material dwells on more emotionally rousing events. Among the *wogul dou* are accounts of aggressive encounters, cruelty, and despair. The trickster Pomapoma (Gwingula), for example, in the course of his adventures, rapes and kills his young mother-in-law in a story which at once deplores his reprehensible actions and presents them in quasi-humorous style. In western Arnhem Land, in a more clearly moralizing or threatening vein, Yirawadbad, in his venomous snake form, kills both his young betrothed wife and her mother because the girl consistently rejected him; he is now dangerous to everyone, but especially to girls, and he makes his reason explicit as he surveys the two corpses. In his human form, he went on to be one of the main instigators of the important Ubar ritual; this includes ritual enactment of the scene where, as a snake in a hollow log, he bites the hand of each woman in turn."[12]

The complexity of native Australian mythic materials, which vary considerably from locale to locale, impedes facile generalizations about the significance of this amorality. Berndt herself notes that scholars have not produced any obvious explanation of whether such materials are meant to discourage, prevent, or deflect similarly wicked behavior in human beings, or whether the myths are more cathartic. Regardless, the difference from Christian views of sacrality is instructive, and certainly a Catholic spirituality, no matter how sympathetic to aboriginal intentions, has to remain confident that the divinity revealed in Christ is light in whom there is no darkness at all.

Human behavior certainly is not light in which there is no darkness at all. Moreover, human imagination, loosed in dreams and reveries, is equally ambivalent, so deep in the human psyche is the awareness of good and evil as distinct possibilities. In their free choices, human beings may follow the light or skulk in the darkness. In what happens to them beyond their choice, through the operations of nature or other people, human beings experience that life may turn either sour or sweet. So there is a temptation to think of existence as bi-polar or dual. At its heart, the human condition may seem poised between equally powerful forces of good and evil. The great dualistic systems, such as Zoroastrianism and Manicheanism, depend on this fear that darkness and light are equi-primordial. Even when they show, by proclaiming a way out of the grasp of evil, that they do not consider the two sides equal, much in Zoroastrianism and Manicheanism wants to place both darkness and light in the depths or formative layers of reality, outside of human beings' control.

Christianity may not be able to explain evil, except as a negativity or privation (lack of proper order and goodness), but it wastes no time in declaring that evil has no hold on God. Certainly, clever minds may tease from scriptural texts doubts about the purity of the divine will, but the overwhelming message of the Christian Bible is that God is utterly reliable. It could not be that the Christian divinity would act from bad motives. It could not be that jealousy, or rage, or wicked desire would deflect the Father, or the Son, or the Spirit from the love that is the Christian's best index of "God." So Christian spirituality stands against systems that worry about the nature or intentions of ultimate reality. In faith, beholding the visage of Christ, it tries to rest assured that in all dealings God is utterly good.

Native Australians probably found their own routes to a confidence about divinity sufficient to help them live in peace, but many reports of first encounters between Christian missionaries and "pagans" suggest that liberation from demonic forces was an important appeal of the Christian good news. The victory of Jesus that the missionaries proclaimed made him the Lord of all principalities and powers. If there had ever been valid grounds for doubting God's control of history, in the triumph of Jesus such grounds washed away. The flood of divine love churning in the death and resurrection of Jesus made plain for all with eyes to see that God wanted only to save the world from its own mortality, folly, and wickedness. As much as divinity could, the Christian God had freed human beings so that they could receive the divine nature and love. The freedom intrinsic to being human required that divinity wait on human choices, but the hunger for being, truth, and goodness built into human spirituality ensured that the odds would always favor a proper use of human freedom.

When one listens to the wisdom of tribal elders from areas such as aboriginal Africa, the lesson taught regularly is that ultimate reality is more wonderful than the uninitiated could imagine. For native Australians, the true meaning of human existence has been to enter more and more deeply into the "dream time" that lays out the splendors of creation and so the immense significance of human existence. If one generalizes from such a conception of human existence, one finds that many oral peoples have sensed far better than their literate successors why human fulfillment must be spiritual.

Certainly, Christians are bound to stand up for the goodness of creation, of the human body, and so of the project to create cultures that follows. Certainly, the flesh of the Word incarnate and the sacramentality of church life reinforce this conviction. But that does not negate the ancient human conviction that wisdom is more precious than any material possession, nor the ancient human hope that, as one ages and experiences more of life, wisdom will come as a wonder at the goodness of God. Yes, wisdom may also suggest the sinfulness of humanity, which alone explains its so frequent blindness to the goodness of God or rejection of the divine overtures of love. But the stronger theme tends to be that life-time is precious in the measure that people think of it as a chance to sojourn with the divine mystery, which is with humanity and creation only as it chooses to be (for love and service).

In this perspective, nothing need separate human beings from God, their fulfillment, because both success and failure point to the divine mystery—either to its benevolence or to human beings' need of its purifications and healings. In this perspective, the stories of sacral forces that make them seem immoral slip away, dismissed like a child's nightmares. Yes, they can teach us useful lessons about the dangers lurking all around, but, for Christian faith, they easily do more harm than good. For it is harmful to fear that reality itself, the substratum of history and final arbiter of human experience, may be warped or antagonistic. It is harmful to doubt that divinity can be anything but gracious —the Father that Jesus staked his entire being upon. So in any dialogue with religious traditions that seem to cast the goodness or purity of divinity into account, Christians have to say, after all proper reminders of the depths of depravity that can produce rampages or holocausts, that everything finally reposes in parental hands, guided or allowed to develop only for the final enrichment of God's people.

NOTES

1. Mircea Eliade, A HISTORY OF RELIGIOUS IDEAS, vol. 1 (Chicago: University of Chicago Press, 1978), p. 26.

2. See, for example, John Cassian, CONFERENCES (New York: Paulist Press, 1985).

3. Marija Gimbutas, THE LANGUAGE OF THE GODDESS (San Francisco: Harper & Row, 1989), p. xx.

4. Lawrence E. Sullivan, ICANCHU'S DRUM (New York: Macmillan, 1988), p. 26.

5. Miguel Leon-Portilla, ed., NATIVE MESOAMERICAN SPIRITUALITY (New York: Paulist Press, 1980), pp. 103–104.

6. Joan Halifax, ed., SHAMANIC VOICES (New York: E. P. Dutton, 1979), pp. 74–75.

7. Elisabeth Tooker, ed., NATIVE NORTH AMERICAN SPIRITUALITY OF THE EASTERN WOODLANDS (New York: Paulist, 1979), p. 107.

8. Ibid.

9. Mircea Eliade, ed., FROM PRIMITIVES TO ZEN (New York: Harper & Row, 1967), pp. 269–270.

10. Colin Turnbull, THE FOREST PEOPLE (New York: Simon & Schuster, 1962), pp. 106–107.

11. Mircea Eliade, ed., FROM PRIMITIVES TO ZEN, p. 130.

12. Catherine H. Berndt, "Australian Religions: Mythic Themes," in THE ENCYCLOPEDIA OF RELIGION, ed. Mircea Eliade (New York: Macmillan, 1987), vol. 1, p. 560.

Chapter 3

Hinduism and Buddhism

Vedic Sacrifice

At the foundations of Hinduism, the sacred culture of the Indian subcontinent, lies a fusion of two prior cultures. The fertility interests of the native peoples, who focused much of their attention on the earth, merged with the concern of the invading peoples (the Aryans) to dominate reality with the help of heavenly forces. The Vedas, the most sacred Hindu scriptures, are our best indication of the wonder and reverence that accompanied the Aryan desire to understand and control reality. As Vedic religion unfolded, a priestly caste came to preside over many rituals, and with time ritual sacrifice became the center of Aryan culture. Through sacrifice the people might control the gods—not merely honor them but bend them to a human will, so that they would supply everything that earthly existence required. Along with this development of ritual sacrifice went an intellectual development: the desire to get to the bottom of the plethora of forces in the world and find their underlying unity.

In the following text we catch the ancient Hindu mind at a point where sacrifice and the desire to grasp the ground of reality had joined: "Brahman is the priest, Brahman the sacrifice; by Brahman the posts are erected. From Brahman the officiating priest was born, in Brahman is concealed the oblation. Brahman is the spoon dripping fatness; by Brahman is the altar established. Brahman is the essence of the sacrifice; the priests prepare the oblation. To the minister, praise!"[1]

Brahman is the name that early Hindu thinkers gave to the ultimate cause and substance of reality. In the Upanishads, the poetic meditations one finds at the end of the Vedas, the view emerges that Brahman is everything. For example, one cannot separate the *atman*

51

that animates human beings from Brahman, because in the final analysis they are one. If a European thinker were working out this equation, the operative word might be "being." Being is one everywhere, because everywhere anything that is real exists or is. The Hindu Brahman has a more personal tone, yet it is also impersonal—the being or ultimate "stuff" of everything. Thus, in these verses from a sacrificial prayer, one finds that Brahman has taken over all the roles in the play.

In an earlier part of this Veda the poetic author had spoken of divinity sacrificing to itself: "There where the Gods made an offering to the Gods, where, immortal, they worshiped with heart immortal, may we also revel, in highest heaven. May we gaze on it in wonder at the rising of the sun!"[2] Here the deduction is complete: Brahman does and is everything. When one looks below the surface, all action and honor belong to divinity. The prayer is quite concrete: the priest, the sacrifice, the posts, the oblation, the spoon, the altar—when one asks about the foundations or inmost substance of any aspect of the ritual, Brahman stands forth.

Christianity has its own version of this "pantheism," though to use that word triggers alarms. Because it holds to a doctrine of creation from nothingness, which Hinduism by and large does not, Christianity separates creatures from their creator more drastically than Hinduism does. Moreover, because it believes that Jesus Christ was a unique, or at least uniquely definitive, incarnation of the creator, Christianity relativizes the divinity of lesser presences of God. They bear forth aspects of divinity, but only Jesus Christ *is* God literally. Of course, Hinduism speaks of many incarnations (*avatars*) of divinity, but such speech tends to occur in the context of devotional theism, where the focus is a god such as Krishna or Shiva. Here we are concerned with the presence of divinity throughout creation, natural as well as human.

The Christian sense of the divine presence avoids pantheism by qualifying all of its predication about the immanence of divinity. Even in the case of the incarnation of the Word, leading to the strict divinity of Jesus the Christ, orthodox faith is quick to add the balancing notion that Jesus was also fully human, and that because of this full humanity his divinity could seem, could in some ways be, limited. Following out all the twists and turns necessary to articulate a precise yet fully contemporary christology is the business of professional christologists and so not our task in this book. We need only note that even when Christians affirm the full divinity of Christ they have to retain a proper modesty, because of the union of that divinity with a complete and so in many ways limited humanity.

The more pertinent reflection is the Christian conviction that nothing exists apart from God, and that God shepherds all creation providentially. Christians could not use the language of this Vedic hymn in speaking about sacrifice, but they have labored to give all the priority to God. This has meant noting the movement of the Holy Spirit in the depths of the faithful, whence their prayer would arise with sighs too deep for words. It has meant keeping a bifocal view of the eucharistic sacrifice, such that Christ could be both priest and victim. And, more generally, it has meant applauding the instinct of contemplation that God may be found everywhere, because everything is an effect of the divine creativity and love.

If Hindus using the Vedas tried to shore up their hopes that their sacrificial prayers would be heard, would become efficacious, by noting how divinity had to be at work in all aspects of the sacrifice, Christians using biblical formulas have tried to do much the same. The psalms offer many textual bases for begging the Lord himself to make efficacious the sacrifice that prayer implies. The typical Christian sacramental ritual invokes the Holy Spirit and hopes that the participants' praise will rise to heaven with the Spirit's help—on its wings, one might say.

But the more that Christian prayer developed, the more that somewhat external imagery such as that of a sacrifice by people below to divinity above tended to fade. The presence of God in grace meant that heaven had come to earth, that divinity was at hand soliciting a mutual knowing and loving. Certainly, "heaven" remained different from earth, and so something to which the faithful could aspire. Certainly Christ seated at the right hand of the Father suggested all that remained to be accomplished, before his return to overcome the difference between heaven and earth. But the substance of heaven, intimacy with God, was at hand. "Grace" has meant the very life of God, which surpasses even God's forgiveness and acceptance.

So the Christian equivalent of the Vedic wonder at the omnipresence of Brahman turns out to be the indwelling of the Holy Trinity. Father, Son, and Spirit, "come" to take up their abode as the gospel of John promised, cast the inmost identity of the believer, the recipient of divine life, in terms of a knowing and loving that are truly divine. Yes, one should hasten to say that this divinity is only by adoption—is not the natural divinity found only in Christ. Yes, one should recall that only the great mystics knew enough about the experience of diviniza- tion to explain how it works like the consummation of a marriage. But simply on basic theological grounds, working with familiar scriptural texts and creedal assertions, one has to agree that Christians can and should speak of a God more intimate than our deepest sense of selfhood, more pervasive than the air we breathe.

Truly, in God we live, move, and have our being. Truly, the light that flashes when we understand, the warmth that courses when we love, is the operation of divinity in us. In virtue of Christ, none of our operations is "merely natural." All of our bodily being is blessed, and all of our spiritual being is carried by the spirituality of God—the being, knowing, and loving that constitute the Trinity. So an analogue that can make Christians coming to the eucharistic sacrifice like Vedic Hin- dus gazing in wonder at the rising of the sun (a regular time for sacri- fice) is the conviction that faith bestows not just a dim knowledge of God but a participation in God's own life. When sacrifice is the coin of divinization, it makes the self-giving love of Christ a template for all of humanity's intercourse with God.

Upanishadic Wisdom

We can describe the goal of contemplation in many ways, but one dear to many contemplatives, east and west, is as a path to wisdom. By contemplating ultimate reality, and opening ourselves to its revelations, we may come to see rightly, realistically. When we do, the truths of tradition that we accepted in trust become things we understand some- what—things that have a sweet savor. The kind of wisdom touted in religious circles is experiential, not academic. However sharp or learned the mind describing it, the gist of the wisdom itself is a fusion of light and warmth, of knowledge and love. Only such a fusion is strong enough to persuade people that divine revelation, rather than sensual imagination, is the teacher to follow. Only a loving knowing and know- ing loving satisfies the whole longing of the human heart and so can seem a foretaste of heavenly fulfillment.

The Katha Upanishad offers a stimulating view of how many Hin- dus have thought about wisdom (the goal of their contemplations and prayers): "The wise one (the Self) is not born, nor dies. This one has not come from anywhere, has not become anyone. Unborn, eternal, primeval, this one is not slain when the body is slain. . . . He, however, who has not understanding, who is unmindful and ever impure, reaches not the goal, but goes on to reincarnation. He, however, who has understanding, who is mindful and ever pure, reaches the goal from which he is born no more. . . . When are liberated all the desires that lodge in one's heart, then a mortal becomes immortal! Therein he reaches Brahman! When are cut all the knots of the heart here on earth, then a mortal becomes an immortal!"[3]

The seat of wisdom, according to this Upanishad, is the atman at the core of the human being. As the presence of divinity (inseparable from Brahman), the atman partakes of the divine nature, neither being born nor dying. When ancient Indians studied the differences between divinity and humanity, they concluded that humanity is painful because of being born and dying, and so that divinity must not be born or die—must simply be (in bliss and awareness). The divinity in human beings, responsible for their animation and intelligence, stands apart from the bodily conditions under which human beings experience it. (One can say that yoga attempts to escape from these conditions and so afford an unconditional experience of divinity or ultimate reality.) When people understand this freedom from conditions that lodges in their depths, they can sense that space and time do not contain them. Living without the desire that chains most human beings to space and time, to death and rebirth, they can allow their divinity to take over and free them from the deaths and rebirths that make ordinary human existence excruciating.

This is the famous Hindu doctrine of karma and reincarnation. The Buddha accepted the idea that the key to overcoming suffering is to stop desire, but he worked with or developed a different picture of ultimate reality. For the moment, though, we need consider only the Hindu picture sketched in this Upanishad. On the one hand, it offers a view of the spiritual life that a Christian can find quite admirable. On the other hand, it runs afoul of Christian incarnationalism and so seems to put obstacles in the way of Hindu-Christian accord.

Admirable is the goal of union with divinity, or the process of divinization, that the text spotlights. Plato spoke for the Greek expression of what seems to be an Indo-European ambition: to become as much like God as possible. Christianity baptized Platonism and interpreted this ambition in terms of God's prior drawing of the human being through grace. What the human striving to understand ever more deeply and love ever more completely seeks, God has given in superabundant measure through the indwelling of the Trinity—the assumption of the believer into God's own inner life of knowing and loving.

Certainly there are many steps on the way from Plato, let alone the Katha Upanishad, to the Christian doctrine of divinization by trinitarian indwelling, and there are many distinctions that one should make. But something in the structure of the search remains parallel in all three cases: the Hindu, the Greek, and the Christian. Each stems from an intuition, husbanded by experience, that humanity is fettered until it engages with a divinity that takes it outside of its finitude, mortality, and (for Christianity) sinfulness. The secret to human fulfillment is the desire that keeps springing up, until human beings find a truth, a love, that overwhelms their vast but still limited capacities. How to deal with this desire is a key question for any spirituality, and Christians have much to learn from Hindu views of detachment, purification, and renunciation. If John of the Cross and other Christian masters, following up on the strictures of the New Testament about self-denial, taking up one's cross, and following Jesus, and on the experiences of the desert fathers and mothers, can speak of a radical renunciation as the way to the highest union with God, then Christian disciples aware of their tradition should not find Hindu talk about liberation from desire impossible to accredit.

Still, there is the Christian sense that the human being is not merely a material housing for a divine spirit. Both Hinduism and Platonism had a difficult time with the body, because it seemed to be the main obstacle to human fulfillment (which they conceived to be completely spiritual). Despite all the insight that yogins accumulated about the ties between the body and the spirit, the debts of pure thought to imagination, and the suppler life that the body could enjoy, when the spirit had progressed toward liberation, the image of a prison kept coming to mind. Even death was not necessarily a comfort, because death could become merely the gateway to another birth and so round of suffering. Only if the human personality had broken free of karma (here meaning the impediments or attachments caused by desire) could one hope that death would be the occasion for escape to *moksha*—the state of definitive freedom from suffering (and so the state that ultimate reality enjoyed). Thus everything bodily, from birth to death, stood somewhat under a pall, though many Hindus became patient by contemplating the many eons available for gaining wisdom and relief, and basic Hindu ethics considered pleasure (*kama*) more legitimate than blameworthy.

The Christian desire for divinization can and cannot legitimately long to escape from the body. Inasmuch as the body we know seems incapable of full union with divinity, theologians have spoken of a "glorified body," on the model of the physical appearance of Christ after the resurrection. The preferred biblical symbolism for complete fulfillment, resurrection rather than immortality of the soul, also suggests that the body is capable of whatever purifications and transformations divinization requires. So while it is legitimate to long to escape the torpor, ignorance, suffering, and sinfulness that we are bound to associate with physical limitations, it seems the part of truly incarnational Christian faith to transform such longing into images of heaven that include the transformation of the body and incorporate the social dimensions available to us through our flesh (friendship, community life, interactions with nature [a new earth as well as a new heaven]).

Christian wisdom therefore tends to include a reverence for matter, and an unwillingness to write matter off as having no capacity for union with God, that gives Christian spirituality a different feel from the spirituality of Hindus. Perhaps such a difference narrows in practice, where people who pray seem to converge experientially, beyond what their doctrinal orientations might seem to allow. But it would be well for Christians to make sure that their own contemplative wisdom illumined the sacramentality of the body (the lustrous humanity of the Johannine Christ, for example), before they worried about correlating their prayer with Hindu notions of atman, karma, and quenching desire.

Caste

The bugaboo of Hindu social justice, in the eyes of westerners (and now many Indians), is the system of caste that stratifies society. There are four major divisions in this system, and many minor differentiations within each major division. The result is a social system, claiming divine sanction (one of the creation accounts derives the four castes from the division of the original human being), that tilts interactions among people and seems to institutionalize injustice.

Consider, for example, the following description of the duties of the lowest class, that of the workers (Shudras): "I should tell thee, O Bharata, what the duties of a Shudra are. The Creator intended the Shudra to become the servant of the other three orders [priests, warriors, merchants/farmers]. For this, the service of the three other classes is the duty of the Shudra. By such service of the other three, a Shudra may obtain great happiness. He should wait upon the three other classes according to their order of seniority. A Shudra should never amass wealth, lest, by his wealth, he makes the numbers [sic] of the three superior classes obedient to him. By this he would incur sin. With the king's permission, however, a Shudra, for performing religious acts, may earn wealth. I shall now tell thee the profession he should follow and the means by which he may earn his livelihood. It is said that Shudras should certainly be maintained by the (three) other orders. Worn out umbrellas, turbans, beds and seats, shoes, and fans, should be given to the Shudra servants. Torn clothes, which are no longer fit for wear, should be given away by the regenerate classes unto the Shudra. These are the latter's lawful acquisitions. Men conversant with morality say that if the Shudra approaches any one belonging to the three regenerate orders from desire of doing menial service, the latter should assign him proper work. Unto the sonless Shudra his master should offer the funeral cake. The weak and the old amongst them should be maintained. The Shudra should never abandon his master whatever the nature or degree of the distress into which the latter may fall. If the master loses his wealth, he should with excessive zeal be supported by the Shudra servant. A Shudra cannot have any wealth that is his own."[4]

This description is bound to strike the American reader as akin to the view of slaves that prevailed among slaveholders during the nineteenth century. One human being is defined as completely the possession of another. The being of the slave exists only to serve the master. The three "regenerate" classes (members received a sacred thread at their coming of age, to designate their capacity for *moksha*) live on a different plane from that of the servant. Something in the Hindu history or psyche required that social order be grounded on the lesser existence of the workers, whose progress (gaining of better karma) depended on a faithful service of their superiors. They could not hope to become farmers or merchants, warriors or priests, in a future life unless they performed well as workers in the present life.

The notion that one belonged to a given social class and that one had a strong duty to stay in that class, fulfilling the responsibilities that tradition assigned to it, created the important Hindu sense of *dharma*. Dharma could mean the Teaching, the Truth, handed down by tradition, but it could also mean, in a more restricted denotation, the caste duties specific to one's state as a priest or worker. No doubt there was considerable flexibility about such duties, since they had to evolve over time, but even in the present many people in India are keenly aware of the caste into which they were born, feeling that their caste determines many of their options.

Indeed, even in the present those who fall outside the caste system (the untouchables) can suffer terrible discrimination and cruelty. Mahatma Gandhi wanted to liberate the untouchables, whom he called "the children of God," but he was slow to call for the complete demolition of caste, because he knew how deeply rooted it was. Severe contemporary critics, such as the novelist V. S. Naipaul, find the whole matter ridiculous—a blight on the Indian soul. But an historian of religion, even one repelled by the injustices and suffering that caste creates, has to be impressed by the passion for social order that such cultural developments express. Rather than wonder about how to order relations among the different functionaries of society, many peoples have created rigid, even ruthless codes to regulate social conduct. (This is equally true concerning relations between the sexes. In the case of traditional Hinduism, men ruled women even more stringently than the upper classes ruled the Shudras.)

Without denying that much in traditional Hindu culture is bound to remain enigmatic, or that, on their own terms, many Hindus probably found numerous ways not only to make sense of caste but to lessen its deleterious effects, Christians are bound to reflect that their Lord has imposed on them a very different social sense. If one reads the gospels sensitively, it is clear that Jesus challenged all the social distinctions that kept people from treating one another as brothers and sisters or that obscured the equality of all under one parental God. Indeed, the regular diction of Jesus was to bless the poor, the outcaste, the "sinners" (social deviants), because often they were more open to the kingdom of God (Jesus' basic message was that God had drawn near to free humanity from its dead ends) than rich and respectable people were. We recall how the poor fare in the beatitudes, in Mary's Magnificat, and in Jesus' ministry. It is Jesus' regular custom to consort with the poor, or at least with ordinary people, rather than with the wealthy and powerful. Jesus' enemies, predictably enough, spring mainly from the priests and Pharisees whose status he threatens. So in numerous ways we find Jesus becoming a radical social reformer, convinced that the gospel requires a thorough renovation of how human beings ought to deal with one another.

For a Christian spirituality intent on reforming itself in light of today's global culture, this passion for social justice and conviction that all human beings are radically equal could make a distinctive, much needed contribution. Many other religions have profound insights into human sociability, and many demonstrate lovely care for the poor and suffering, but Christian incarnationalism, and Christian discipleship to a suffering master, could make Christian spirituality signal for casting off pomp and circumstance, for taking on the bearing of a servant.

Does this mean that Christians should consider themselves the Shudras of the world, bound to offer themselves up for the prospering of others? Not many Christians would embrace this suggestion immediately. The mentality of the well-intentioned colonist, setting out to instruct the benighted colonized remains alive and well. But if we think about a Christian Shudraship, we can realize why many Hindus were not appalled by the notion of caste. In the best of cases, the workers were not only following the duties assigned to them by divinity, they were also placing in the world a selflessness bound to dispose them well for liberation. Yes, Shudras, like all others, could be consumed by desire. Poverty and subjection are no guarantee that one will rapidly acquire purity of heart—quite the contrary. But Christians admiring the selflessness of their saints have to realize that, of itself, servanthood is more than compatible with the gospel of Christ.

Indeed, Christians have to recall that Jesus defined himself as having come to serve rather than be served. The ministry of Jesus, consummated on the cross, was the expression of his great love for his brothers and sisters. Nothing was more precious than helping them feel, in their bones, that God could care for them. So the work that Shudras have been assigned, and even the subjection that they have suffered as a class, could not keep them from living lives pleasing to God. Reprehensible as their subjection was, on both Hindu and Christian terms divinity could use it for good ends. This is not to accept the pernicious Hindu notion that low caste is a punishment for evil-doing in a previous life, nor to open any door to slavery. On Christian terms, only a radical equality, such that no group dominates any other and none claims superiority before God, honors the gospel. It is simply to say that God is more creative than human beings, so that even when human beings develop terrible social structures God can bring individuals to a holy selflessness and joy.

Manu on Teachers and Parents

The Hindu literature commenting on social relations goes under the name *Dharmashastra*. In addition to the system of caste, a schema for the ideal life-cycle organized many Indian intuitions about social order. The ideal life-cycle unfolded in four phases. First one studied with a guru, living in celibacy and obedience, to learn the sacred traditions. Then one married, raised a family, and lived as a householder, caring for parents and contributing to the commonweal. Third, when one's hair had turned gray and one saw one's children's children, it was time to withdraw from the active life and become more contemplative —both to prepare for death and to revitalize one's sense of the holy traditions, in light of one's experiences of life in the world. Last, if one's contemplation brought enlightenment, one could wander the world as a teacher, giving good example (demonstrating the priority of concern with ultimate matters) and instruction.

The most famous and influential Hindu commentary on social relations goes by the name *The Laws of Manu*. "Manu" is an Adam or First Human Being, whose wisdom, mythically, stemmed from the original time, when the order of the world was clearer than later generations found it to be. According to Manu, the relationship between the teacher and the student is especially holy, and from the following reflections on this relationship we glean some interesting hints of how traditional Hindus thought about some key social relationships: "He who performs the vow (of studentship) shall constantly subsist on alms, (but) not eat the food of one (person only); the subsistence of a student on begged food is declared to be equal (in merit) to fasting. Let him not pronounce the mere name of his teacher (without adding an honorific title) behind his back even, and let him not mimic his gait, speech, and deportment. By censuring (his teacher), though justly, he will become (in his next birth) an ass, by falsely defaming him, a dog; he who lives on his teacher's substance, will become a worm, and he who is envious (of his [teacher's] merit) a (larger) insect. The teacher, the father, the mother, and an elder brother must not be treated with disrespect, especially by a *brahmin* [priest], though one be grievously offended (by them). The teacher is the image of *Brahman,* the father the image of Prajapati (the lord of created beings), the mother the image of the earth, and an (elder) full brother the image of oneself. By honouring his mother he gains this (nether) world, by honouring his father the middle sphere, but by obedience to his teacher the world of *Brahman.* All duties have been fulfilled by him who honours those three; but to him who honors them not, all rites remain fruitless. By (honouring) these three, all that ought to be done by man is accomplished; that is clearly the highest duty, every other act is a subordinate duty. The teacher is ten times more venerable than a sub-teacher, the father a hundred times more than the teacher, but the mother a thousand times more than the father. Of him who gives natural birth and him who gives the (knowledge of) the Veda, the giver of the Veda is the more venerable father; for the birth for the sake of the Veda (ensures) eternal (rewards) both in this (life) and after death."[5]

Characteristically, texts such as *Manu* are compilations from different strands of tradition. Thus, characteristically, they make a given topic the be-all and end-all. So one may take this glorification of the teacher with a grain of salt. On the other hand, religious teaching (and ritual) was a function of the upper caste. If the ruling class (warriors and administrators) were supposed to hold sway in temporal matters, brahmins were supposed to care for eternal, religious matters. That was the basis for their special dignity. Members of the three upper castes were eligible for a life-cycle that began with an intense studentship, but brahmins considered such studentship especially fitting. No man proclaiming himself dedicated wholly to the pursuit of moksha had to marry (and married men who had fulfilled their responsibilities as householders could declare themselves free of further obligations to their wives), but brahmins felt special pressures to embrace for shorter or longer periods the celibacy associated with the pursuit of holiness.

The teacher deserves special dignity because the teacher is the conduit of Dharma. The text makes the same point by associating the teacher with the transmission of the Veda (here meaning roughly the same thing as Dharma: sacred knowledge). Nothing is more valuable than instruction in sacred knowledge, because sacred knowledge is the means to salvation (moksha). The psychology of the ideal Hindu life-cycle is challenging. First it is necessary to apprentice oneself to a teacher learned in the tradition and holy because living by its precepts. But such an apprenticeship is bound to have limited effects, as long as one has little experience of where the tradition came from (why the ancient seers credited with the Vedas saw as they did). As a householder one can learn where the tradition came from. What seems easy or obvious to the diligent student, in the cloistered context of the teacher's compound, becomes both more difficult and more precious when immersion in sexuality, finance, parenting, caring for elders, politics, and general culture show the tangledness of human action and motivation. For example, the counsel to stop desire becomes much more significant.

The need to grade the different influences in a person's life—teacher, father, mother—is characteristic of Indian thought in particular and many ancient systems in general. Indian culture fostered considerable speculation, which led to many different classificatory schemes—for levels of consciousness, types of beings, categories of virtues and vices. At the roots of this schematizing lay the oral culture created between teachers and students. On the whole, teachers taught *viva voce,* explicating a text. The *sutra,* the smallest unit of a sacred text, therefore became like a string on which one hung several memos. Any rhythm, alliteration, ordering, or vividness that made a memorable summary of what the teacher had thought, when he explicated a section of a Veda or a passage from Manu, became precious. Thus the tradition also unfolded in sutra-like form: through pithy, memorable commentaries.

In our verses the main point is to exalt the teacher as the most essential parent, because the teacher begets eternal life in the student, whereas the parents have only begotten temporal life. And yet one text reverses this general tendency, exalting the father over the teacher and the mother over both of them. Whether this is simply a metaphoric interlude, so that the teacher can gain greater clout by being pictured as the true father and mother in the deepest sense, is not clear from our selections. But for the mother to be exalted over the father and teacher, even momentarily, cracks the patriarchal cast of the social system that we have dealt with to this point, reminding us not only that real households could differ considerably from ideal ones, but also that the Great Goddess (*Mahadevi*), collecting to herself the entire assemblage of feminine qualities and powers, has long been the most popular deity among the common people. So in making the mother a thousand times more venerable than the father, Manu weaves into his design for the social order another ingredient—one potentially capable of calling in doubt all of its hierarchies. If the female is both the most honored member of the household (because of her ties with generation) and the most dangerous (other texts portray her as requiring constant control by males), then the entire social schema is up for grabs.

Christians are likely to rejoice at such a possibility, inasmuch as Christian instinct prefers the Spirit of God to the dead letters that overly formalistic social schemes can be. The Spirit of God breathes where it wishes, now exalting men and now exalting women, now spotlighting the teacher and now spotlighting the parent. Ironically, of course, Catholicism has its own tendency to schematize social relations, not least of all in the church. The same dynamics that led brahmins (who tended to control the interpretation, if not the production, of sacred texts) to glorify the priest and teacher led many church leaders to glorify bishops and priests. On the one hand, the sacred functions of bishops and priests justify glorifying them. On the other, all glory belongs to God, in the best Christian schemata, and God can raise up children of Abraham from mere stones. So before they disparage Hindu formalism, noting its close ties with social prejudice, Christians ought to contemplate the prejudices that have prevailed in their own history, blushing that so often they also have been more concerned with power than with service and holiness.

Buddhist Mindfulness

Buddhism developed on Indian soil. The Buddha was an heir of the Vedas and a contemporary of some of the Upanishads. When he set out to solve the problem of suffering, long-standing traditions of meditation lay ready to hand. Thus it was no accident that Buddhism developed as a religion that stressed meditation, as well as morality and the guidance of the community. One of the stages or preoccupations of the Eightfold Path that the Buddha laid out for his disciples was mindfulness, which helped to shape the practice of Buddhist meditation. As a venerable sutra records the master's teaching on this point: "There is this one way, monks, for the purification of beings, for the overcoming of sorrows and griefs, for the going down of sufferings and miseries, for winning the right path, for realizing Nirvana, that is to say the four applications of mindfulness. What are the four? Herein, monks, a monk lives contemplating the body in the body, ardent, clearly comprehending it and mindful of it; likewise the feelings in the feelings; likewise mind in the mind; likewise mental states in mental states so as [to] control the coveting [of] dejection in the world. And how does a monk live contemplating the body in the body? Herein, monks, a monk who has gone to a forest or the root of a tree or to an empty place, sits down cross-legged, holding his back erect, and arouses mindfulness in front of him. Mindful he breathes in, mindful he breathes out. Whether he is breathing in a long or a short breath, he comprehends that he is breathing in a long or a short breath. Similarly when he is breathing out. He trains himself, thinking: 'I shall breathe in, I shall breathe out, clearly perceiving the whole (breath-) body; I shall breathe in, breathe out, tranquillizing the activity of the body.' "[6]

We note in passing that Buddhism has been no less inclined to tidy schemata than Hinduism, and that the yogic strain in both traditions has often focused so directly on the body that in practice any antagonism toward the body could leech away: if the body could be such a helpful focus, on the way to enlightenment, one could not disparage it wholeheartedly. Coming to more central matters, what is mindfulness? Attention. Concentration. Overcoming distraction so that one lives in the present, undivided, focused on the matter at hand. Note that mindfulness is not an end in itself (although in some schools, such as Soto Zen, masters could speak as though it were—as though enlightenment could express itself through mindfulness, removing any need to strain in search of a breakthrough to enlightenment). For this present sutra (attributed to the Buddha), mindfulness is a powerful means to the great end of overcoming suffering and gaining full liberation (nirvana —the Buddhist equivalent of moksha). If the monk (from the beginning the inner circle of Buddhism has been the monastic community, living in celibacy, begging alms, and spending much time on meditation) will concentrate on the body, the feelings, the mind, and the mental states, managing to dwell within them while examining them (managing to allow no subject-object dichotomy in his study), then mindfulness will grow and draw to it the wisdom of enlightenment.

To become mindful of the body in the body, yogins often utilize the breath. The breath mediates between the spirit and the body. If one follows one's breath mindfully, dwelling within it as it flows in and out, being aware of it without being detached from it, then one will move

toward the state from which enlightenment springs. The posture speci-
fied in the text is a time-tested way of stimulating alertness and produc-
ing the integration of mind and body that mindfulness both requires
and enhances. The thought that mindfulness wants to develop is a
simple observation of what is. The trick, very difficult for most begin-
ners, is to persevere with this thought, dwelling within it. Typically, the
mind of the beginner squirts away, so that he or she cannot say, "I shall
breathe in, I shall breathe out" (perhaps better: "I am breathing in, I
am breathing out"). Typically, the very simplicity, the very non-
dualism, proclaimed in this beginning exercise comes to seem a mark of
perfection.

Before shifting to Christian reflections, we need only suggest how
mindfulness correlates with the wisdom, the insight into the true nature of reality, that is both its goal and its underlying support. Buddhist
wisdom is much concerned with an immediate perception of how
things exist, how things are. Pain and suffering, it believes, flow from
desire, which causes us to grasp at things and denature how they are.
We do not perceive them correctly or interact with them beneficially
because we have prejudgments and agendas. Our minds are whirring
with projects that we want to accomplish, satisfactions that we want to
gain. So we cannot let reality be.

Mindfulness, and other aspects of Buddhist meditation, aim at
putting us in psychosomatic states where it is easier to let reality be. As
we become accustomed to such states, become adept at them, we may
realize that reality "is" nothing solid, permanent, isolated. Reality is not
the bundles of independent beings or things that our schemata for
organizing the data of sensation and our ideas about the world make us
think it is. Reality actually is flowing, interdependent, and selfless.
There is no ultimate entity behind a reality divided into bits and pieces.
There is no personal self, no "I," separating me from the rest of reality
and making me static or substantial. There is only the dance, as T. S.
Eliot put it. Mindfulness would insert us into the dance, help us move
along with the stream that is always flowing.

Much of this is so different from the language used by Christian
masters of prayer that it seems to come from a different world. And, to
be sure, the personal character of the Christian God, the Christian
stress on love, the Christian demand for social justice, and the absence
of anything remotely approaching a yogic program in the teaching or

personal bearing of Jesus all suggest that the initial impetus of Christian spirituality was quite different from that of Buddhism.

On the other hand, Christians now believe that God has been present to all people's hearts. They now realize that any programs or disciplines that seem to produce holiness—honesty, depth, goodness, humility, social service—deserve an attentive hearing. It may remain true that Christian contemplation must finally find focusing on the breath, or the body, or the feelings an impediment or sidetrack, rather than a straight path to love of God. But this judgment can simmer, waiting upon more living contact with Buddhists who find that their meditations open them to a reality both beautiful and healing. Indeed, this judgment can wait upon further reflection on the negative strain in Christian mysticism, where divinity seems to appear in the mode of darkness, nothingness, a reality so simple and seamless that one best appreciates it by simply paying attention. This appreciation would have to be interpreted as a mode of love, if it were to qualify as quintessentially Christian prayer, but perhaps it could be—love of the being, the plain "isness," that divinity has made its most basic presence.

Buddhist Devotion

One of the simple distinctions between Theravada and Mahayana Buddhism, according to many manuals, is that Mahayana admitted more devotions geared to the laity. On examination, this distinction both holds up and seems to be simple-minded. For it is true that Mahayana Buddhism developed more dramatic ways for the laity, rooted in the world, to make love of the Buddhas (now multiplied, as if to cover more psychic needs) a path to liberation, but it is also true that Theravada Buddhism, supposedly more austere, found devotionalism present in the teaching of the Enlightened One from the beginning.

Consider, for example, this Pali text, from the scriptures dear to Theravada: "There are these four places, Ananda [the Buddha's favorite disciple, and so frequently the interlocutor in sutras], which the believing man [person] should visit with feelings of reverence and awe. Which are the four? The place, Ananda, at which the believing man can say, 'Here the Tathagata [Buddha] was born!' is a spot to be visited with feelings of reverence and awe. The place, Ananda, at which the believing man can say, 'Here the Tathagata attained to the supreme and perfect insight!' is a spot to be visited with feelings of reverence and awe. The place, Ananda, at which the believing man can say, 'Here was the kingdom of righteousness set on foot by the Tathagata!' is a spot to be visited with feelings of reverence and awe. The place, Ananda, at which the believing man can say, 'Here the Tathagata passed finally away in that utter passing away which leaves nothing whatever to remain behind!' is a spot to be visited with feelings of reverence and awe. . . . And they, Ananda, who shall die while they, with believing heart, are journeying on such pilgrimage, shall be reborn after death, when the body shall dissolve, in the happy realms of heaven."[7]

Textual criticism, little practiced in traditional Buddhism, would probably suggest that these verses came from considerably after the lifetime of the Buddha and represent practices in place for generations since his death. Otherwise, the Buddha is looking forward to what will happen after his death—not an impossibility for an Enlightened One, but something that textual critics, operating on humanistic criteria, are bound to consider unlikely. Regardless, the fact is that the birthplace of the Buddha, the place where his enlightenment took place, the place where he preached his Dharma (the translator seems overly influenced by Christian terminology in speaking of the Buddha's establishing a kingdom of righteousness), and the place where he died became sites of pilgrimage (even when no one could be sure precisely where such sites lay, in the actual history of the man Gautama).

The reason for this impetus to pilgrimage is not hard to find. Human beings need things of flesh and blood to anchor their religious hopes. It pleases devout Buddhists to frequent what they think is the birthplace of their hero and Lord, as it pleases Christian tourists to Bethlehem. The Bodi Tree, under which, tradition says, Gautama vowed to remain until he had reached enlightenment, is somewhat like Calvary in the career of Jesus: the place of supreme test and victory. The kingdom of righteousness may be the Dharma that the Buddha preached or his establishing of the Sangha, the (monastic) community that became one of the three main "refuges" of the Buddhist faithful (where they put their trust). Finally, the site of the Buddha's *parinirvana* (entrance into nirvana) is like Mount Olivet, the place from which Jesus passed into heaven. Both Buddhists and Christians have considered pilgrimage to sites supposedly significant in the historical career of their Lord a meritorious work, particularly in times (like the Christian middle ages) when people took religious traditions quite literally.

These glimpses into the foundations of Buddhist pilgrimage and popular religion remind us that, however lofty its philosophical doctrine or meditational practice, Buddhism felt obliged to accommodate itself to the needs of the common people—even to the needs of the credulous. Christianity has shared this feeling. It would be better for the simple faithful to err on the side of credulity, Christian and Buddhist leaders seemed to agree, than to lack vivid supports for their faith. Our text is clear that only those who believe in the Buddha will find sites of great events in his life venerable. It also is clear that the merit pilgrims can gain from visiting such sites is limited: no promise of nirvana, only promise of entry into high heavens (better karmic states) after death. Still, by contemplating what occurred at the revered site in question, a faithful Buddhist might stir the feelings of gratitude and rededication that could motivate him or her to renew the pursuit of higher virtue.

Catholic spirituality, somewhat in contrast to Protestant, has always tolerated devotion to the saints and even credulous wonder about the true cross of Christ or the Shroud of Turin (supposed to be the burial cloth of Jesus). So clear was the Catholic instinct that Jesus had to be wholly flesh and blood, completely one of us human beings in his humanity, that it formed a spirituality fraught with personal feelings about the love, goodness, pain, and other aspects of Jesus' life. Through such personal feelings, believers might so associate themselves with their Lord, especially in his sufferings, that nothing would separate them from him.

Buddhist spirituality, generally cooler toward its Lord, less emotional, provided nonetheless for some of the same emotions when it opened the door to pilgrimages to holy sites associated with the Tathagata. Even though the name "Tathagata" is rather abstract, calling to mind the "suchness" (simple being) of ultimate reality and associating the Buddha with it, when this name became common in devotional Buddhism, it accepted charges of affectivity. In Hinduism such charges have been called *bhakti,* which itself signifies devotional love (usually of a personal deity, such as Krishna). Buddhists have shied away from bhakti, not liking the erotic overtones it could carry, but in effect they have sanctioned a kind of bhakti, because they have invited the faithful to engage their hearts with the man Gautama and let their emotions revel in the places he made especially holy.

The lessons for a Christian spirituality wanting to address a world pluralistic in its religious commitments may be to be franker about the humanity of the Christian founder, and not blush about the quite human love that this has called forth. Certainly, sophisticated Christians can laugh at the superstitions that folk customs have introduced into much Catholic devotion. Certainly, they should wish to purify their faith of practices tending to distort it. But they can also humble themselves enough to acknowledge that finding holy places, holy relics, holy memories of a hero's exploits edifying is common to many religious traditions and so seems to express a common or basic human need. Muslims seek such edification through stories about Muhammad and devotions to great saints. Jews have developed pious legends about great rabbis. If such devotional practices remain open to the greater mystery of God, serving as springboards to surrender to this greater mystery, there is little finally objectionable in them.

Problems arise only when someone makes fidelity to the Baal Shem Tov, or the legends about the birth of the Buddha, or the revelations given by the Virgin Mary at Fatima necessary for salvation or orthodoxy. Then right believers in the tradition have to reassert the difference between essentials and accidentals, things that have to be accepted and things that may be taken or left. What has to be accepted is the adequacy of the core message of the founder or revealer in question. What may be taken or left are the accretions, the idiosyncratic devotions, that have arisen from time to time. The core revelation always makes the divine mystery patent and paramount. Advocates of the idiosyncratic devotions, sensing their peripheral character, tend to inflate them out of proportion and so invite deflation.

Monastic Morality

If we try to place the development of Buddhist ethics within the framework of Hinduism, we see that Buddhists capitalized on the freedom accorded monks (those pursuing enlightenment full-time) to prescind from many implications of caste. Admittedly, Buddhist texts such as the *Dhammapada,* a much loved early ethical treatise found in the Pali canon, reflect Indian assumptions about the nobility of the brahmin, making "brahmin" a synonym for "the virtuous person." But disciples were free to join the Sangha, regardless of their caste (the Buddha himself had come from the second, warrior caste), and in time the Sangha admitted women (some traditions say that the Buddha agreed to this only reluctantly).

The monastic life at the core of early Buddhism assured that ethics would develop in tandem with views of meditation and wisdom. In the following description of the ten precepts incumbent on those taking monastic vows, we see the original Buddhist instinct that social justice depends on religious renunciation: "abstinence from destroying life; abstinence from theft; abstinence from fornication and all uncleanness; abstinence from lying; abstinence from fermented liquor, spirits and strong drink which are a hindrance to merit; abstinence from eating at forbidden times; abstinence from singing, dancing, and shows; abstinence from adorning and beautifying the person by the use of garlands, perfumes, and unguents; abstinence from a high or a large couch or seat; abstinence from receiving gold and silver. [These are] the ten means (of leading a moral life)."[8]

The context of these precepts is an ordination ceremony carried out in 1872. A British writer, invited to attend, published an account of the ceremony in the *Journal of the Royal Asiatic Society* in 1874. But the content and spirit of these precepts have solid roots in Buddhist tradition. For example, the first five precepts have long been incumbent on all Buddhists, laity as well as monks, constituting the fundamentals of what Buddhists call *sila* (morality). Not to kill, steal, lie, be unchaste, or drink alcohol has been a handy, negative summary of the call to practice non-violence (*ahimsa*), be detached about possessions, revere the truth, maintain sexual purity, and keep a sober, clear consciousness.

Through the centuries, Buddhist ethicists tended to gloss these precepts, much as Christian ethicists tended to gloss the ten commandments. Although the first focus was private morality, it was not hard to develop social implications. For example, Buddhists wanting to improve working conditions, or health care, or the chances for peace could elaborate the first precept so as to picture careless employers, negligent doctors, and military leaders as offending against it. The precept against theft could be extended into rules for how to conduct banking, the expropriation of land, and the use of materials for scholarship. The first five precepts dealt with such basic matters that they showed all Buddhists what the elementary implications of the Buddha's pathway had to be. "Right conduct," another of the stations on the Noble Eightfold Path (we have already considered mindfulness), turned out to include both a proper regard of oneself and a proper regard of other people.

To be unchaste, for example, was to violate the integrity requisite for enlightenment, but it could also be to involve others in one's disorder. To become drunk was to pollute the instrument of enlightenment, one's consciousness, but it could also be to injure other people, at the least by giving bad example. So even though the five basic precepts of *sila* addressed the individual Buddhist, their social implications came to mind quite readily. As well, Buddhists who thought about the conditions necessary for a flourishing community tended to regard these five precepts as the minimal requirements for developing people who might help one another along the Buddha's way (who might make the Sangha a true refuge, a reliable guide).

The last five precepts were not incumbent on the laity but special to monks. They reflect the ordered life that most monasteries tried to establish, and the decorum expected of monks. Monks were to keep the times of silence, live an austere life, be obedient to superiors, and in general flee the world (where ambition, self-concern, greed, and other forms of desire flourished). The precept against acquiring ostentatious furniture gives us a glimpse into the psychology of monastic life, where small marks of distinction, or small creature-comforts, can bulk large.

Christians know about the monastic life, of course, because it has flourished for perhaps eighteen hundred years under Christian auspices. As soon as the Christians who fled to the desert for more intense communion with God began to think about the conditions necessary for success in such a venture, they started to outline what became the foundations of later monastic rules. Their general judgment was that most people required the help of more experienced seekers if they were to persevere and not go astray. The literature associated with the desert fathers and mothers is more moralistic than theological, reflecting the early notion that monks and nuns were in combat with their own lower natures and Satan. The silence, abstinence, and frequent prayer that dominated their lives opened them to serious temptations, as well as to the wonderful grace of God. Only the truly humble would survive such temptations, so many authors made humility the key to virtue.

The quarrel that many Christians have with monasticism, Christian as well as Buddhist, is that it came to seem to slight the implications of loving one's neighbor as oneself. Those implications include working to make the world truly humane, and they only grow when one makes nature neighborly. By the New Testament accounts, Jesus certainly prayed, going off into solitude, and Jesus was poor, chaste, and obedient in ways justifying the monastic development of vows of poverty, chastity, and obedience. But Jesus did not make himself singular, and he spent most of his time teaching and healing. He wandered as need and inclination moved him (Christian monks have divided on the question of wandering, some thinking dedication to a stable community essential), and he was accused of being a drinker and reveler.

So Christian monasticism has had a different relation to its founder than Buddhist monasticism has had to the Buddha. The Buddha lived like a monk (after a wealthy youth and some years of marriage). He was ascetic (though he preached moderation), and he stayed detached from politics. He lived to a ripe old age (about eighty, according to tradition), and his death (due to food poisoning) was more peaceful than that of Jesus, who was executed as a criminal. The Buddha was much more respectable than Jesus, much less the political threat or social critic that Jesus became. Certainly the Buddha's teaching has the potential to undermine all worldly social arrangements, inasmuch as it attacks the desire that stirs so much economic and political activity. But Buddhists have felt less driven than Christians to heal the sick, help the poor, defend the powerless. Many Buddhists have done these good things, but Buddhism itself has not received from its founder the charge that Jesus gave to his community (by his example even more than his preaching).

When Buddhists argue that the first step to social justice is the enlightenment of individuals, Christians may agree. But Christians also have to say that their scriptures make social justice a direct obligation from God. Both Jesus and the Hebrew prophets who preceded him, giving him much of his social program, preached that God wants mercy and fair dealing, that God despises the greed and power politics that crush the poor. So a Christian spirituality faithful to Jesus has to press beyond precepts about self-control to explicit calls for social justice. Until Christians consider their wealth, time, and talents as more than personal possessions, as given to them for the sake of their sisters and brothers, they cannot face their Lord comfortably. They ought to discuss this obligation with their Buddhist counterparts, when dialogue focuses on the requirements of a viable spirituality in a world full of hunger and pain.

Political Counsel

The following text implies that the Buddha thought that good social life would follow, if people could meet in concord: "Once the Lord was staying at Rajagaha on the hill called Vulture's Peak . . . and the Venerable Ananda was standing behind him and fanning him. And the Lord said: 'Have you heard, Ananda, that the Vajjis call frequent public assemblies of the tribe?' 'Yes, Lord,' he replied. 'As long as they do so,' said the Lord, 'they may be expected not to decline but to flourish. As long as they meet in concord, conclude their meetings in concord, and carry out their policies in concord . . . as long as they make no laws not already promulgated, and set aside nothing enacted in the past, acting in accordance with the ancient institutions of the Vajjis established in oldest days . . . as long as they respect, esteem, reverence, and support the elders of the Vajjis, and look on it as a duty to heed their words . . . as long as no women or girls of their tribe are held by force or abducted . . . as long as they respect, esteem, reverence, and support the shrines of the Vajjis, whether in town or country, and do not neglect the proper offerings and rites laid down and practiced in the past . . . as long as they give due protection, deference, and support to the perfected beings among them so that such perfected beings may come to the land from afar and live comfortably among them, so long may they be expected not to decline, but to flourish.' "[9]

The implication of this counsel seems to be that the Buddha's instinct was to support solid tradition and focus on community accord. Assuming that the traditions of a people (here the tribe known as the Vajjis) are sound, the soul of political prosperity is to honor them. When the people as a whole do so, agreeing that they show the way forward, the community knows what it is and how it is to proceed.

What place is there in such an outlook for innovation and progress? Who is to say that the ancient traditions are the best, or that they are not responsible for significant injustice? Is any people ever so fortunate that it does not require new ideas, better mousetraps? These are the questions that a modern reader is bound to entertain, and reflective

Buddhists might find similar ones rising, if they remarked on the fact that the Buddha himself was an innovator. Rejecting the Hindu traditions of his day (or at least the prevailing interpretation of those traditions), he launched a new venture, confident that the truth he had discovered on his own could heal the sufferings of many other people. Why should the Buddha have denied to others the right he claimed for himself—the right to innovate, in the name of improvement?

This is an interesting, relevant question, but of course it will have to remain speculative, since we cannot summon the Buddha to testify on his own behalf. The answers that we might put in the Buddha's mouth ("What I learned was an objective truth, valid for all people, about the structures underlying all searches for liberation. By comparison, questions of political arrangements are of minor importance, and experience shows that innovation tends to do more harm than good. So while I offer a revolutionary spiritual stance, my politics are conservative") remain more our own than his.

After having noted that many religious founders wanted to preserve as much of their contemporaries' cultural milieu as possible, lest those contemporaries plunge into chaos, we can conjecture that this instinct was at odds with the new ideas that the founders brought, so that it was only a matter of time before the religion in question was creating new political, artistic, economic, and other arrangements. For example, even though Jesus is reported to have wanted to preserve the Torah, not removing a jot or tittle, before long it became clear that his followers had serious differences with their fellow Jews, because they wanted to open the covenant to the Gentiles. From ideas of Jesus and his message came political and cultural consequences. Did the words of the Buddha suggesting the maintenance of traditional customs prevent his followers from political and cultural innovation?

By no means. The most famous Buddhist king, Ashoka, left a record, almost a brag, describing reforms that his conversion to Buddhism created. Taking Buddhist ideas about non-violence and virtue to heart, he tried to restructure his kingdom and create a regime consonant with Buddhist peace. More broadly, as Buddhism moved to the east it interacted with non-Indian cultures, changing some of them significantly and being changed by them in return. For example, Chinese and Japanese Buddhism differ from Indian Buddhism significantly, and both China and Japan absorbed so much from Buddhism that they are perceptibly different from what they were prior to its

advent. Buddhist missionaries may have thought that they were bringing the unchanging Dharma and merely translating it into new culture
forms, but such differences as the East Asian preference for the concrete led to startling changes in both doctrine and practice. The Chinese receiving Buddhism may have thought that it would simply invigo-
rate their native traditions, but because Buddhism brought such new
ideas as reincarnation, people's views of death, the afterlife, and present
social interactions were bound to change.

The analogy for Christian faith and spirituality is obvious, though
its bearing on social justice may not be. Christian missionaries have
done best when they sought to make Christian faith indigenous to the
people they approached. Trusting to the Holy Spirit, and the good will
of native converts (trained as well as possible), the best missionaries
have rejoiced in the rise of a native liturgy, theology, catechesis, and
ethics. The history of Christian missions shows that the greatest stum-
bling block to progress has been an insistence on retaining Latin, or
western thought-forms, or a single liturgy. Nowadays the decline of
Christianity in the west, and its rise in the east and Africa, suggest that
the future of the gospel lies with non-European groups. The handwrit-
ing is on the wall: unless the church is able to strike a graceful balance,
making sure that the substance of the gospel does not wander from
what the New Testament and the core tradition portray but allowing
sufficient freedom for this substance to animate local cultures, it will
not be a good householder, faithful to its charge to bring forth treasures
both old and new.

The question of social justice implied here is first of all a matter of
equality within the Christian community itself. Granted a proper respect for the history of Christian faith, so much of which has been
European, why should European cultural forms have higher standing
than Indian, or African, or Chinese, or Brazilian? Certainly it is a difficult, perhaps an impossible task to determine how much cultural
"translation" changes the substance of the Christian message, but the
earliest Christian missionaries, such as Paul of Tarsus, were confident
that the Holy Spirit would supply.

In this context, such "short formulas" of Christian faith as those
developed by Karl Rahner are immensely helpful, because they focus
the debate about what the substance of the gospel in fact is.[10] Adapting
an ancient dictum, we can say that there must be unanimity about
necessary things, there should be liberty regarding doubtful things, and

in all matters there should be charity. Rahner's formulas imply that the necessary things are few, the doubtful things are many, and so great liberty should prevail. Indeed, his formulas imply that God alone can supply the understanding that missionary theology wants to communicate, because in the final instance God's is the work of convincing hearers that Jesus has words of eternal life available nowhere else. To believe in the God of Jesus, and make Jesus one's key to interpreting human existence, one has to experience the love poured forth in human hearts by the Holy Spirit. If the Spirit is no respecter of persons, but tends to enter wherever people open their hearts, then there should be a radical equality among the cultures to which the church tries to preach the gospel, in the midst of which the church tries to be the great city lifted on a hill to show all people the humanity God wants for them.

NOTES

1. Atharva Veda, 19:42:1–2, in Raimundo Pannikar, THE VEDIC EXPERI-ENCE (Berkeley: University of California Press, 1977), p. 360.

2. Atharva Veda 8:5:3, in ibid., p. 359.

3. Katha Upanishad, 2, 3, 6, in THE HINDU TRADITION, ed. Ainslee T. Embree (New York: Vintage Books, 1972), pp. 64–65.

4. Mahabharata, 12:60, in ibid., pp. 82–83.

5. Manu, II, 188, 199, 201, 225, 226, 233, 234, 237, 245, 246, in A SOURCEBOOK IN INDIAN PHILOSOPHY, ed. Sarvapalli Radhakrishnan and Charles A. Moore (Princeton: Princeton University Press, 1957), pp. 178–179.

6. Majjhima-nikaya I, 55–58, in BUDDHIST TEXTS THROUGH THE AGES, ed. Edward Conze et al. (New York: Harper Torchbooks, 1964), pp. 56–57.

7. Mahaparinibbanasutta, 5:16–20, 22, in BUDDHIST SUTTAS, trans. T. W. Rhys Davids (New York: Dover, 1969), pp. 90–91.

8. Henry Clarke Warren, BUDDHISM IN TRANSLATIONS (New York: Atheneum, 1973; orig. 1896), p. 397.

9. Digha Nikaya, 2:72 ff., in THE BUDDHIST TRADITION, ed. William Theodore de Bary (New York: Vintage, 1972), p. 48.

10. See Karl Rahner, FOUNDATIONS OF CHRISTIAN FAITH (New York: Seabury, 1978), pp. 448–600.

Chapter 4

Chinese and Japanese Religion

The Analects *on Sacrifice and God*

For well over two thousand years the ethics of East Asia has been Confucian. Scholars tell us that Confucius did not seek to innovate, but only to hand on the traditions of the ancient Chinese sages, so it may well be that "Confucian" ethics in fact is more than three thousand years old. Scholars tend also to regard Confucian ethics as humanistic: what Chinese experience reported about the best way to achieve harmony with the cosmos, within the state, for the family, and in the individual. So persuasive was this ethics that eventually it entered into the marrow of Japanese, Vietnamese, Korean, and other Asian cultures.

But what does the word "humanistic" mean in this context? Are the scholars who want to distance Confucianism from anything religious correct? Much depends on semantics—how "religion" is to be understood. On Christian grounds, where the human being is so made for God that nothing significant occurs without evoking the divine mystery, there is no humanism (in the sense of an understanding or love separated from divinity). Indeed, on Christian grounds everything about the human condition is graced: solicited by God to open itself to divine love. That Confucius himself had some inkling of the inevitability of dealings with divinity seems plain from several statements in the *Analects,* a collection of his sayings put together by his disciples. There one finds that Confucius thought it very important for the gentleman (the sort of human being he was trying to cultivate) to know the ancient, traditional rituals intimately and participate in them from the heart. There one also finds that Confucius thought it important to be on good terms with "Heaven," a symbol that ancient China, like many other ancient cultures, used for the numinous powers overseeing human affairs.

78

So, when we try to estimate the roots of traditional Chinese spirituality, we do well to contend with texts such as the following: "Of the saying, 'The word "sacrifice" is like the word "present"; one should sacrifice to a spirit as though that spirit was present,' the Master said, If I am not present at the sacrifice, it is as though there were no sacrifice. Wang-sun Chia asked about the meaning of the saying, 'Better pay court to the stove than pay court to the shrine.' The Master said, It is not true. He who has put himself in the wrong with Heaven has no means of expiation left."[1]

The first saying summons a problem central in all spiritualities: how to pay attention. We saw this problem in Buddhism when we dealt with mindfulness. Any Christian recognizes it from discussions about distractions in prayer. Here Confucius is at his usual station, fielding questions from his students. Many of the questions amount to requests to explain traditional sayings. Like ancient Indian wisdom, ancient Chinese wisdom did business by summarizing venerable lore in pithy sayings. The assumption was that teachers and students would mull over these sayings, in the give and take of live instruction. The ancient lore regarding sacrifice was that it so depended (for its efficacy) on attention that one could find the word "present" in the word "sacrifice." (Chinese ideograms allowed considerable leeway for conjecture about the historical evolution of a given character.) Sacrifice was an offering to a spirit, and so a quasi-interpersonal exchange. If one did it mechanically, or without paying attention, it was useless, because the spirit would be offended, or at least not moved to help. So this saying assumes the typical ancient worldview, in which spirits were lively, and human beings, very conscious of their fragility, sought constantly to get helpful spirits on their side and keep harmful spirits at bay. Just as one had to pay attention, if one were to hunt well and avoid omnipresent danger, so one had to pay attention at one's sacrifices, because there the stakes were just as high.

Confucius agrees with the spirit of the traditional saying. If he is not present, attentive, when the sacrifice occurs, for him there is no sacrifice. He might as well not have attended, not bothered to engage with the spirits or traditions involved. This response gives the lie to the charge that Confucianism was a mere formalism. Perhaps it degenerated to that on occasion, but at its origins the Master sought to infuse all sacrifices and rituals with personal involvement and commitment. When the king officiated at the spring rites, begging the powers of heaven and earth to grant fertility to the land and the people, all good members of the realm were with him in spirit, begging at his side. The efficacy of the rites was not mechanical. It depended on a populace sufficiently human (immersed in its traditions) to appreciate what was being transacted and petition the spirits wholeheartedly.

One can respect the humanistic interpretation that makes this ideal a function of social consciousness (the desire of every people to develop a unity of mind and will), but this begs a further question. How does social consciousness relate to ultimate reality—the powers that surround human consciousness and seem to hold its fate? On their own terms, most ancient peoples have thought that their identity was inseparable from the gods they served, the spirits they petitioned. Ancient China was no different, so one cannot reduce its civil sacrifices to exercises in social togetherness. That is not how any public consciousness, least of all a mythological one (as all ancient cultures were) operates.

The second saying is even more to the point. Confucius is offered the chance to dismiss religious rituals as irrelevant and plump for pragmatic concerns, and he rejects it out of hand. The stove represents workaday business, domestic needs, what we might call secular interests. The shrine represents divine, spiritual, transcendent interests. Confucius laid great stress on practical wisdom—prudence and knowledge of human affairs. But he realized that all the practical wisdom in the world cannot control the larger forces of life and death, good fortune and bad. That is why the ancients whom he revered had developed their various rituals and put great stock in them. The rituals were occasions for the people to recognize their contingency, exorcise the anxieties it was bound to rouse, and petition the sacral powers for help. Confucius respects this wisdom and makes it his own. If we are in the wrong with Heaven, we have no other recourse. We cannot save ourselves, and our many failings require expiation. Attending only to pragmatic affairs, even those incumbent on us because of family responsibilities or good citizenship, is not enough. We must deal directly with the powers whom we offend, when we violate the ways of the cosmos or disfigure our consciences.

Christians approaching the wellsprings of an ancient culture like the Chinese with a strong conviction about the presence of divine grace everywhere are bound to admire these Confucian convictions. In fact they may interpret these convictions as indications that Confucius knew that conscience itself is holy, and that each significant claim upon conscience is a claim from God. But there is more to the texts than this. There is also an expression of the natural religiosity of the human spirit, its inherent tendency to wonder about the powers holding its existence and bow before them reverently.

When he participated in the traditional rites, Confucius would bow low, abasing himself before superior powers. He would offer his gifts in the spirit of a subject petitioning a majesty, or even of a penitent begging forgiveness. Stuffy and proper as he might be in his human dealings, his punctiliousness at the rites could express the concern of a creature well aware of its utter dependence on those who had guided its life to the present—those who controlled all forces and fates. And so his desire to be fully present to the sacrifice could bespeak a hunger to do right by his God, however implicitly or inarticulately this desire lodged in his heart (because his culture had not differentiated the notion of a personal creator who had fashioned the world from nothingness). This is the generous possibility we favor in dealing with Confucius, as with all worthy non-Christians, so this is the scenario that most pleases us.

The Successful Ruler

When Confucianism became the state orthodoxy, furnishing the imperial government its political philosophy, a canon of quasi-sacred writings emerged. These were all attributed to the Master, who had become a divine sage (himself worthy of sacrifices). People aspiring to civil service pored over the canonical texts, because they were the basis of the examinations that determined acceptance into the civil service. How much this instauration of Confucianism as the state's mental apparatus diluted the original liquor of the Master himself is hard to say. At the least, we can be sure that such radical notions as "the mandate of heaven" (prominent in the writings of Mencius, the most influential apostle of Confucian thought) got a tame interpretation.

The mandate of heaven was the approval that heaven gave to a given political regime—its ultimate legitimation. The assumption was that a given dynasty possessed the mandate of heaven, because heaven allowed it to rule. Since the emperor was the high priest of the people, their crucial link with heaven, through whom order passed from above to below, it was repugnant to think that a ruling dynasty could be illegitimate. On the other hand, when a dynasty lost power and was overthrown, people said that heaven had withdrawn its mandate. The Confucian interpretation of such a loss was that the rulers had failed to move the people by moral persuasion. Confucius was opposed to rule by force. In his view, only the good example of the ruler, the ruler's manifest expression of the goodness of heaven, stabilized a regime for the long run. If the people loved their ruler and felt solidarity with him (occasionally queens ruled China, but that was exceptional), the realm would run well.

The Confucians derived this conviction from such ancient documents as the *Book of Songs,* as we see in the following passage: "The *Book of Songs* says, 'How the people are pleased with their ruler, who is like a parent to the people.' The ruler loves what the common people love and hates what the common people hate. That is how to be a parent to the common people. Again the *Books of Songs* says, 'Oh, the magnificent Southern Mountains! How majestic are the rocks! How magnificent is the Grand Tutor Yin! The people look up to him.' Thus those in a position of authority should never be careless; once they go wrong, the whole world will denounce them."[2]

The bulwark of virtue in the Confucian scheme of things is filial piety. When children revere their parents, the home is in good order, and when the home is in good order the state flourishes. Within the family, the father holds most authority. Women are to obey men, just as younger sons are to obey older sons. The obedience that the people owe their ruler is like the obedience that children owe their parents, or that students owe teachers. All is quite hierarchical. What saves the hierarchy from blind obedience and makes it work is the virtue of those in authority. Let the father really be a father, and the children will obey from the heart. Let the teacher be wise and good, and the students will study zealously. And let the emperor, or any other ruler in question, be wise, fair, self-sacrificing rather than self-aggrandizing and the people will stay in line, will even be enthusiastic about carrying out the imperial will.

In the ideal case, a straight line of goodness and obedience runs from heaven to the smallest child in the lowliest peasant family. Heaven offers the ruler good reason to be virtuous (to follow the ancient mandates and pursue harmony with the sacred cosmos). The ruler attuned to heaven offers the people (nobles, merchants, peasants—all classes) good reason to obey the imperial edicts. The family led by a virtuous father falls in line and participates in the peace, the harmony, that heaven desires. Certainly each peasant has immediate access to heaven and the spiritual realm, but for human institutions a hierarchy mediates the divine will.

The Confucian conviction that virtue, manifested in good example, is the key to a peaceful and prosperous political realm clashed with other schools, such as that sometimes known as "The Legalists," which favored rule by strong laws and punishments. At issue were two different conceptions of human nature. Confucius thought that human nature was sufficiently good to make rule by moral example effective, though he was not so optimistic as Mencius, who thought that *jen* (benevolence) was built into human nature. The Legalists thought that human beings would only toe the mark if they were frightened and compelled. This argument has raged in many other cultures, and there is no settling it by appeal to facts or experience. What ought Christians to think about it, and how ought spirituality, virtue, and politics to cohere in the Catholic scheme of things?

If we study the primary Christian documents, giving pride of place to the gospels, we find that Jesus did speak of laws and punishments, but that he subordinated these to an appeal to love. His Father still carries overtones of the lordship and judgeship prominent in some parts of the Old Testament, but a parental love is more central. Jesus himself sought no political power to enforce his message. He did not want the arm of the state aiding his cause. His sole strength was moral (or, more precisely, religious) persuasion: consider the depth, rightness, beauty, and relevance of my message. Consider the works that I do, in witness of its power.

Implicit in this appeal is a trust of human nature and a reliance on human freedom. Yes, Jesus was disappointed in human beings on occasion, and the gospel of John says that he did not trust the enthusiasm of the crowds, because he knew about human nature (its fickleness, presumably). When the children sing their song, "We played you a jig and you would not dance, we sang you a dirge and you would not mourn," the evangelist's appropriation is bitter: there was no pleasing Jesus' contemporaries. It was perversely fitting, though not inevitable, that he would end up on the cross.

And yet this realistic assessment of human perversity does not make Jesus long for military power. On the testimony of the Christian masters of the spiritual life, it does not lead God to force people to prayer or love. God continues to move as divinity did in the person of Jesus: gently, like a kind parent or even a vulnerable lover, rather than a harsh Lord.

Can one translate this interpretation of religious experience into a political philosophy that relies on holiness (that is, exceptional love) rather than laws and punishments? The Christian spirituality that we see aborning says yes—that is the only way viable in the future. The weapons of destruction are now so lethal that military force is a dreadful option. Many groups long oppressed have become aware of the violence done them and will tolerate it no more. And human beings truly come of age, truly aware of the legitimate advances of modernity, realize that they cannot obey God, or their human rulers (secular or religious) like children, bowing to rules and controls they do not understand.

God seems to rejoice in this desire for maturity, even when many religious and political rulers do not. Otherwise, why would God have staked so much on free responses, on human beings' giving back love for love? To have the spirituality, the humanity, that Christian faith finds in the mind of God, the exchanges have to be free and loving. One cannot compel holiness or even virtue. One has to persuade people that they can risk themselves as love requires, that it is sensible to make the sacrifices on which virtue depends. In this light, Jesus stands as the great effort of God to persuade humanity of the divine love.

As they pondered this question, many of the saints concluded: What more could God have done? Divinity took flesh, to share our lot to the bone. Divinity suffered and died on our behalf, to rescue us from sin and death. And divinity offers us divine life, fulfilling our most ardent hopes at a level beyond our wildest expectations. All of this is free (a matter of grace). None of it had to be or stems from a necessity in God. None of it compels us or takes away our power to say no. So all of it ratifies the best Confucian intuitions, taking them to another plane. For Christian conviction, that is what faith in Jesus sees regularly: an elevation of the best that human beings have glimpsed anywhere, so that, purified, it reposes in God.

Chu Hsi on Love

Confucians had their own keen sense of how everything reposes in such ultimate principles as heaven and earth. Remarkably, they also had their own convictions about the priority of love. Thus Chu Hsi (1130–1200), the great synthesizer of Confucian thought (the Chinese Thomas Aquinas), wrote a treatise on love (*jen*) that began as follows: " 'The mind of Heaven and Earth is to produce things.' In the production of man and things, they receive the mind of Heaven and Earth as their mind. Therefore, with reference to the character of the mind, although it embraces and penetrates all things and leaves nothing to be desired, nevertheless, one word will cover all of it, namely *jen* (humanity). Let me try to explain fully.

"The moral qualities of the mind of Heaven and Earth are four: origination, flourish, advantages, and firmness. And the principle of origination unites and controls them all. In their operation they constitute the course of the four seasons, and the vital force of spring permeates all. Therefore in the mind of man there are also four moral qualities—namely, *jen*, righteousness, propriety, and wisdom—and *jen* embraces them all. In their emanation and function, they constitute the feeling of love, respect, being right, and discrimination between right and wrong—and the feeling of commiseration pervades them all. Therefore in discussing the mind of Heaven and Earth, it is said, 'Great is *ch'ien* (Heaven), the originator!' and 'Great is *k'un* (Earth), the originator.' Both substance and function of the four moral qualities are thus fully implied without enumerating them. In discussing the excellence of man's mind, it is said, '*Jen* is man's mind.' Both substance and function of the four moral qualities are thus fully presented without mentioning them. For *jen* as constituting the Way (Tao) consists of the fact that the mind of Heaven and Earth to produce things is present in everything. Before feelings are aroused this substance is already existent in its completeness. After feelings are aroused, its function is infinite. If we can truly practice love and preserve it, then we have in it the spring of all virtues and the root of all good deeds."[3]

Several aspects of this exposition seem startlingly Christian. First, there is the notion that the ultimate principles (divinity) permeate everything and give everything its inmost character. Second, there is the notion that the mind of ultimate reality is reflected in human minds. Since "mind" does not mean simply the intelligence, but implies rather the total awareness, emotional as well as intellectual, this notion is equivalent to the biblical idea that human beings are images of God. Third, there is the idea that the key feature of divinity is origination—creativity. Heaven and Earth are the principles from which everything comes. Fourth, there is the idea that the quintessence of the human reflection of such origination is *jen*. In its several connotations—humanity, love, commiseration—*jen* is the seat of human creativity. Thus, if one wants to develop all the virtues (all the excellences that creation holds out, all the possible imitations of divinity), one should study *jen*, work at *jen*, make *jen* the treasure on which one's heart is set.

For present purposes, perhaps we do best by focusing on the ties between natural creativity and human flourishing implicit in these lines from Chu Hsi. The social justice incumbent on the global spirituality required in the future will have to embrace the natural world, the total environment. So the rather impersonal cast of the Confucian divinity becomes a useful stimulus.

People raised on the Bible have not appreciated the impersonal presence of divinity throughout nature as well as they might have. The polemics of the Bible against idolatry have obscured the fact that nothing flourishes or fails apart from God's grant of existence—God's ongoing creativity. Certainly, the story of Israel's covenant with God, which was like nothing so much as a troubled marriage, preoccupied the Old Testament writers and inclined them toward personalist categories. Certainly the story of Jesus' redemptive mission only heightened this personalism. But without backing away from the Christian conviction that the essence of the drama enacted through the millennia of human existence has been God's loving work to give human beings divine life, Christians nowadays can appreciate better the natural backdrop of this drama. Nowadays we can see more clearly than the biblical authors did that God is present everywhere, loving everything into being.

Creation and redemption are not disparate activities or histories for God. The revelations that human beings most prize, which come through feelings and images of interpersonal love, are not foreign to the revelations that come through appreciation of the beauty and power of non-human creation. The divine life that God offers to human beings is a light and love that explodes the stars, stirs the genetic codes, jostles the tectonic plates. We limited beings cannot understand how an awesome impersonal power can cohere with the most tender and intimate love, but God embraces both peacefully. If we reflect on the Confucian sense of *jen*, we may enter upon a greater share of God's peace.

Many of the Christian saints have thought that the primary presence of divinity lies in the depths of the human spirit. Thus Augustine and John of the Cross have stressed interiority as the way to God. The appeal of this way is its intimacy. Take the most tender, touching human encounter, focus on how it moves into the heart and soul, and then credit God with the fullest measures of the exquisite tact you find. There is God the lover, the spouse, accomplishing what every profound friendship or romance longs to achieve: complete union. With God, finding one's lover and finding one's self coincide perfectly. Within the Trinity, and within the human personality brought to divine union, lover and beloved define themselves mutually.

Certainly, there is no equality between the human beloved and the divine lover, the divine beloved and the human lover. But God supplies equality sufficient for friendship and espousal to occur. God makes our prayer to God. The Spirit (God given and received in our hearts) so represents us before God or carries us into divinity that in loving us God can love God, as God has always to do. That is the power of the interior way: it shows us, in the categories that bring us the most delight, the categories of love, that we can only define ourselves, let alone fulfill ourselves, through an exhaustive love of God (God's love for us, but also our love for God—both of which have no limit and leave no remainder).

This is more romantic than what Confucianism suggests, but it does not violate the Confucian intuitions about the presence of Heaven and Earth in all things, originating them, and the primacy of *jen*, the virtue (force) that makes us human. Chu Hsi does not say that divine origination is a function of divine *jen*, no doubt because he is intent on making *jen* the crux of humanity, but he implies that origination and *jen* are parallel or mirrored. So, we may think that the best analogue of *jen* in Heaven and Earth, the best "translation" of the divine origination that explains the world, is a force of love and commiseration. Throughout the natural world that was traditional China's first sense of reality or creation, divinity is bringing things into being through love and commiseration.

The love is striking enough: a regard for rocks and trees, a parental pride and care for seas and mountains. But the commiseration is so striking as to seem impossible: surely what separates divinity from human beings is that divinity does not suffer. Surely the analogy breaks down, because nature shows so little pity. But then, if our reasoning is permeated by a sense of traditional Christian spirituality, we may recall that God's ways are not our ways, and that such a recall is a two-way street. We should not assume that God can only love us in ways that are gentle and pleasing, and we should not assume that God's apparent impersonalism, whether in nature or in our own lives, is not a species of love, even of care.

What we have to assume, out there at the end of our religious imaginations, where our spit of insight plunges into the ocean of God, is that God asks and deserves a *carte blanche*. Though he slay us, yet must we trust him. Though we can't see how cancer or human betrayal can mediate God's love, we can believe that it does. We can believe, and so love, beyond what we can know. God can be God, fully loving and saving, in ways that we cannot feel. Chu Hsi may have had none of this in mind when he reflected on the relations between divine origination and human love, but thinking his thoughts after him in tandem with Christian faith can bring it all to center stage: all of the drama of creation, natural and human, is a function, a play, of the divine being, which is the divine love.

Lao Tzu

A century or so after Confucius, the ideas now associated with the name Lao Tzu crystalized enough to supply an alternative to Confucian humanism. Lao Tzu is apparently more legendary than historical, and the ideas at the origin of his school, Taoism, are poetic to the point of considerable malleability. One can find in the *Lao Tzu* (also known as the *Tao Te Ching*) pretty much what one wants. Generally, however, interpreters agree that the cast of mind is more naturalistic than what one finds in Confucian texts (more absorbed with the Tao [Way] that moves through creation). Also, the cast of mind is more passive or detached. The Taoists are the great debunkers of busyness, pushiness, thinking one knows it all. They remind us that no law works except by depending on a virtue that law itself cannot guarantee. They note that the key to survival is to keep one's head down, one's profile low, and flow along with the stream. The great Taoist virtue is *wu-wei:* not-doing, sensitive restraint, delicate seconding. Stereotypically, then, Taoism is feminine, while Confucianism is masculine. Confucianism wants to act and move things around. Taoism wants to react and let natural harmonies sing.

This does not mean that Taoism is emotional—sticky with concern for victims and underlings. Indeed, one of the most famous texts from the Lao Tzu seems to proclaim just the opposite: "Heaven and Earth are not humane (*jen*). They regard all things as straw dogs. The sage is not humane. He regards all people as straw dogs."[4]

This text seems to contradict what we found in Chu Hsi's essay on *jen*. Lao Tzu will have no truck with the notion that the ultimate powers act (or think, or feel) as human beings do. Does this mean that the ultimate powers are heartless, even cruel? Not necessarily. It simply means that they are not partial the way that human beings tend to be. They do not take family ties or friendships into account, at least not to the extent of making them direct how nature is to run, who is to get sick and who is to stay well.

The straw dogs were pieces used for ceremonial rites. The Way, or Nature, has no more regard for creatures than people organizing a party have for the decorations they use. Such people need not wreck the decorations, but they will seldom cuddle up with them. The decorations, the straw dogs, have a function, and those employing them are satisfied if they fulfill their function well. So does the sage (here meaning one who knows how nature runs, with special implications for how to handle human beings politically) regard the people. He is not partial. He does not become emotional. He is detached, independent, aware of bigger pictures. The appeal of the people is their brute being and need. The sage does best when he allows this appeal to help him guide the people in the way to harmony with nature (harmony with the apparently inexorable way that things are).

Can this be the philosophy that drew Thomas Merton, that was the womb of much Zen Buddhism, that has delighted readers the world over (some say that the Lao Tzu is the most translated book in the world)? Yes, in the sense that from such detachment or naturalism came great freedom, humor, and insight into the paradoxes of human existence. This may become clearer when we deal with Chuang Tzu, a more dazzling writer than Lao Tzu, but the charm of Taoism is strong in Lao Tzu as well.

The Taoist is more drawn to the valley than to the mountain, to the infant than to the adult, to the female than to the male, to the water than to the rock. Century by century, the water wears away the rock. In household after household, the infant dominates the adult, through its need. The valley is not lashed by the storm as the mountain is. The ·female lives longer than the male and more often gets her way (or better learns to make her way realistic). It is amusing that so many bright people, intent on success, overlook these elementary truths. It is striking that so many study the outside of the house, its structure, and forget that the inside space is what makes a house valuable. Which is the tree that survives through the years? Not the handsome straight one. That is admired by carpenters and soon becomes planking. It is the gnarled, ugly tree that survives. It is the quiet, unobtrusive servant, domestic or civil, who rides out changes in administrations and keeps his limbs intact (chopping off a hand or a foot was a typical punishment for malfeasance or disloyalty).

These piquant observations are not inhumane, but they are detached and unsentimental. The mind from which they spring, in which they enjoy favor, is used to gazing unblinkingly at human folly. Before the law codes proliferated, Lao Tzu thinks, there were no criminals. Before the dawn of "progress," people slept well. When you are well rooted in nature, you become like an uncarved block of wood or stone. Little of your potential has been destroyed. An original integrity is still in place. The Taoists wanted to preserve and cultivate the uncarved block: original human nature, before civility had weakened it.

If we join these notions with our prior discussion of the freedom of divinity to meet or not meet our human expectations, we find that Lao Tzu has his own brand of negative theology. The Tao is not necessarily what human beings expect. Ultimate reality is more quirky, creative, volatile. One cannot capture nature in a picture, or a law, or a technique. Yes, these convictions came from a premodern time, when human technology was limited. Yes, they run afoul of modern success in natural science, which has formulated many useful laws. But they remain salutary reminders that much has not changed. Not only do the laws of natural science not render up the full intelligibility of nature (not only does nature remain mysterious: too full for finite intelligence to hold), individuals still experience their personal fates as casual—a throw of the dice. So whatever grain nature shows, and however much Taoists wanted people to work with that grain, life has continued to be fraught with disharmonies (or to play its most significant harmonies in frequencies that we cannot hear). The best that one can do is to live in a joyous detachment. The sanest stance is to have no dogmas, no rigidities, no sureties.

But in the kindly interpretation that we have been attempting throughout this interaction with the history of religions, such postures can seem wonderful confessions of the godness of God. When Christians say that the Father is unoriginated, they confess that all origination, pattern, providence, and the like stem from God, and that none of them captures God. God is the source and holds all the primacy. Creatures are derivative and so secondary. The secondary moves at the behest, to the music, of the primary. That continues to be so, even when the secondary is human and tries to use its freedom to thwart what it takes to be the will of the primary. Whether the creature can thwart the will of God is a nice question in Christian theology—the razor's edge of the mystery of how divine providence and human freedom mesh. But under the stimulus of Lao Tzu one sees all the reasons for thinking that God can never be thwarted, and so one sees some of the reasons for thinking with Julian of Norwich that all manner of thing will be well.

Chuang Tzu

As noted, Chuang Tzu (also both a text and a legendary person) espouses the same basic ideas as Lao Tzu but writes more engagingly. He is, for instance, dramatic about the processes of change, which emerge most clearly at the time of death. Consider, for example, the reactions of Masters Yu and Ssu when Master Yu fell sick: " 'Do you resent it?' asked Master Ssu. 'Why no, what would I resent? If the process continues, perhaps in time he'll [the creator'll] transform my left arm into a rooster. In that case I'll keep watch on the night. Or perhaps in time he'll transform my right arm into a crossbow pellet and I'll shoot down an owl for roasting. Or perhaps in time he'll transform my buttocks into cartwheels. Then, with my spirit for a horse, I'll climb up and go for a ride. What need will I ever have for a carriage again? I received life because the time had come; I will lose it because the order of things passes on. Be content with this time and dwell in this order and then neither sorrow nor joy can touch you. In ancient times this was called the "freeing of the bound." There are those who cannot free themselves, because they are bound by things. But nothing can ever win against Heaven—that's the way it's always been. What would I have to resent?' "⁵

This sense of the endless circuits of change, and of the constant transformation of matter from one form to another, is characteristic of naturalistic cultures. Watching the regular circle of the seasons, observing the passing of one generation and the rising of the next, peasant peoples have often developed doctrines of transmigration or reincarnation. Chuang Tzu is not doing that here. There is no indication that he thinks a spiritual part travels from one housing to another, or that Master Yu will be reincarnated as a rooster. His fancy is more mundane: the corpse of Master Yu will decay, nourish the soil, and thereby be transformed into other species of life. Matter and life are ever-moving, always in process of transformation. The ancient Chinese text known as the *Book of Changes* (*I Ching*) ended up in the Confucian canon, but its roots lay in the naturalistic outlook that shaped Taoists such as Chuang Tzu.

The practical effect of this outlook is clear in our text. If we accept the process of change and our present place in it, neither sorrow nor joy will touch us. This may seem a rather stoic achievement, but when one reflects on the vulnerability of ancient peasants, it is nothing mean. Chuang Tzu implies that the happiest life is neither depressive nor manic. The wisest person stays in the middle, peaceful and content. In the middle, one can see things realistically: time is short, protesting one's situation is usually useless, peace of soul is both more attainable and more satisfying. If we have few illusions, we have little to lose. Illusions are to the soul what possessions or baggage are to the body. Invest in them, let them preoccupy your heart, and only sorrow will follow.

The stoicism involved here is more than flatly humanistic. Finally at issue are the dispensations of Heaven. The changes of the seasons, and the changes of state that creatures go through, derive from the will of Whatever is running the world. Chuang Tzu does not doubt that Something is running the world. The Tao is too manifest, too wondrous, to be disputed. Those willing to go into themselves ("shut the doors," Lao Tzu said) can find the Tao to be a highway for spiritual travel. Detached, in freedom, they can soar like the great birds, getting an overview. In overview, the world is ever-changing, but not haphazardly. Certainly Heaven retains the sovereignty, and so new things may emerge. But most of the time the processes of transformation are familiar: ashes to ashes, dust to dust. What is remarkable is the beauty that the process creates: the great mountains, the delicate flowers, the excellent meal or conversation or sex. The process is far from drab or unrelentingly painful. If one does not cling, stays free, one can see good things on all sides.

So the Taoist could find numerous grounds for not becoming cynical or stoic in a harsh sense. There is such playfulness in Chuang Tzu that his detachment seems to have kept him young beyond his years. He uses the form of dialogue to prick the pretensions of the Confucians, and to insert his wisdom into the tradition of sages instructing students (or arguing among themselves). But permeating the whole of his corpus is a bedrock conviction that human beings are not the measure. Like Plato, he had such a sharp sense of something greater than human beings that his every devastation of human pretentiousness was a hymn to the greater significance of divinity (the Tao, or Heaven).

The Christian notion that God is always greater, taken up by the Jesuits as their motto ("for the greater glory of God"), has not passed from view, simply because modern (or postmodern) westerners seldom speak in explicitly theological terms. One can read the postmoderns (for example, the deconstructionists) as clearing the way for transcendence, even if they protest that this is not their intention. Since every exercise in search of meaning (even those trying to prove that there is no meaning) takes place against a mental horizon from which one hopes that light and order will emerge, every destruction of inadequate proposals about meaning can also affirm the greaterness that an adequate Tao or God (ultimate source of meaning) would have to carry.

The aesthetic equivalent of this intuition or latent argument can be a sense that nothing exists by itself, apart from a flowing whole that places all creatures together. John Casey's fine novel *Spartina* comes to this conclusion, and it seems relevant that the contextual symbolism for the whole novel is the sea, one of the most ancient reminders of the fluidity of creation. Thus Casey's hero, Dick Pierce, moves from a reflection about memory and death to a perception of how all the things in his life flow together: "But that wasn't the only reason he thought of Mary and her father, to worry about how he'd be remembered. Not just for that. It seemed to be to get him to relax about something he'd always known—that they all flowed into each other. All of them set about the salt marsh in the little towns and the houses on the hills—they all got mixed in, they stayed themselves. Permeable, yielding to each other, how could they stay themselves? The notion was as dizzying as the notion that time moved through them, that they moved through time. They changed and changed and stayed the same. They were here, they were gone, they were sometime in time. But if there was no time that mattered but the time that was inside them, then they'd be nowhere."[6]

For Christians, God is the somewhere that is nowhere and that holds the processes by which we keep changing and yet remain the same. The "we" is not only ourselves as individuals, though it vivifies the notion of heaven to think about how individuals might change endlessly (moving forward into the endless beauty of God) without ceasing to be the selves that God first loved. It is also ourselves as creatures—the makeup of the natural world, the world that we know through our bodies and imaginations, through our senses and intuitions. We constitute a whole. Whether that whole grows or lives within what is finally a steady-state is unclear, but our interactions suggest that we are permeable to one another, yet not wholly destructively.

Chuang Tzu stressed the final stages of one phase in a given creature's correlations with others: the moment of death and then dissolution. Casey has stressed the permeations that come through awarenesses of time and the communications of life through sex and conception. The entire matter of how creatures form a whole—an earth, a universe, a providence—is very complicated, and most spiritualities have to make due with moments of intuition, when pain or ecstasy breaks down our customary barriers and shows us some of the many ways in which we are members of one another.

For Buddhists, the result of such intuitions is a wheel of karmic connections. For Christians the result should be dazzling appreciations of what the church fathers called "the whole Christ" or what the Pauline school meant by the mystical body of Christ. Expanded, as an ecological theology insists they must be, to include all of nature in proper ways, such intuitions bring us to the highest sociability or wholeness of all: the communal existence of the Trinity. There, in the ultimate mutuality, the ultimate sharing and compenetration that is the outermost and innermost frame of creation, we realize, in the blankness unavoidable in mystical theology, that "our" is more primitive than "my" and "your." Then we sense that Chuang Tzu was right: Heaven has a place and a purpose for all of us—a place that does not isolate us but unites us into something much greater, much grander.

Taoist Politics

In the *Lao Tzu* we read, "Weapons are instruments of evil, not the instruments of a good ruler. When he uses them unavoidably, he regards calm restraint as the best principle. Even when he is victorious, he does not regard it as praiseworthy. For to praise victory is to delight in the slaughter of men. He who delights in the slaughter of men will not succeed in the empire."[7]

Lao Tzu is not a pacifist. He thinks that there are occasions when one must take up arms. But he also thinks that such occasions already imply a defeat. If things are at such a pass that only weapons will secure or restore order, rulers have already failed. The very notions of "victory" and "defeat" are similarly objectionable. Why was the conflict necessary in the first place? Why did there have to be winners and losers? Are there, in fact, any real winners? Don't we all lose when violence and bloodshed occur?

If these questions, explicit and implicit, came from Christian writers, some critics would probably call those proffering them "bleeding hearts." But they come from detached, unemotional Lao Tzu. His motive is not so much compassion for the sufferings of the people injured by violence as disgust at the stupidity, the lack of wisdom, that violence manifests. For Lao Tzu the best ruler is the least intrusive. When government is going well, the head of state is practically invisible. Thus good government is like cooking fish: the less stirring the better. Intervention, busy mucking about, does more harm than good. This principle is doubly true when it comes to stimulating, or even agreeing to, conflict. Always the sage is reluctant to resort to weapons. At best, conflict is the lesser of two evils. What farmer would rejoice at having had to slaughter his cows? What sane ruler rejoices in destroying people who ought to be his subjects, the objects of his care and leading?

The reason that Taoists found Lao Tzu and Chuang Tzu authoritative is that these authors expressed truths of the spiritual life. The spiritual life is not the life of power-politics, any more than it is the life

of money, banking, and consumption. The spiritual life is the life of
reason and mysticism, the life of creativity and love. When our "spirit"
quickens, we realize that the vast majority of what makes a human
existence worthwhile comes from within. If our affairs are well ordered
within, we can manage most external problems quite nicely. That is the
truth in Nietzsche's dictum that people who have a why can put up
with any how. That is the explanation of Chuang Tzu's detachment in
the face of mortal illness, of Lao Tzu's detachment in the face of
warfare. Mortal illness happens. Warfare is sometimes necessary. But
the deeper question, the more crucial inquiry, is what we are going to
make of such eventualities. For Lao Tzu, the political profit we ought to
gain from warfare is the realization that its occurrence is already a
disaster.

So what about Christian forms of detachment, Christian wisdom
concerning violence? What thoughts ought to pass through the minds
of those anxious to develop a global spirituality, when their globe is
rocked regularly by warfare and all sorts of violence? These are not easy
questions, because the Christian traditions do not speak with one voice.
Though non-violence seems to be closer to Jesus' own teaching and
behavior, those thinking it necessary to use force to combat evil can also
cite texts and authorities. One lesson that Lao Tzu teaches us, however,
is the necessity of reluctance. Like the classical Christian theory of the
just war, the Taoist view makes violence, or simply the use of force, a
last resort.

For Christians, warfare represents a breakdown in diplomacy, a
failure of political imagination and good will, such that human sinfulness comes into depressingly clear focus. As soon as "onward Christian
soldiers" shifts from being a symbol of humanity's constant need to
fight against its inner disorders and becomes a call to actual warfare,
Christian hymnody has become perverse. The same with citations of
the Old Testament in support of supposedly holy wars. Very few wars
have begun with holy intentions, and virtually none has ended without
serious sin. Lao Tzu can shake his head about this, maintaining considerable detachment. The Christian has to shed bitter tears, because every
body lying on the battlefield was an image of God, a person beloved to
Christ.

Christian spirituality cannot substitute for political science, any
more than it can substitute for economics. Because Christian spirituality makes its judgments in light of the divine mystery, it can never be

crisp about human motivation or wisdom in given, concrete circumstances. Again and again it has to confess that it does not know, because
the real questions that preoccupy it have no answers. Why do human
beings find it so difficult to get along? Why is justice, fair-sharing,
mutual respect always an endangered species? "Original sin" is the
theological answer, but this turns out to be an answer with close to no
content. Original sin is a mystery—a way of pointing to the surds that
keep recurring in human history. It suggests that the worst flaws go to
the very roots of human nature, and that they have always been with us,
skewing each generation before it left the nursery. The only solution to
original sin is the grace of God, which Christians believe has abounded
more. When people feel the embrace of divine grace, sinning becomes
unattractive.

     Christian spirituality can say more about grace than about sin,
because grace is something positive, whereas sin is something negative
—a privation of reason and goodness that ought to exist, a radical
disorder. What Christian spirituality has to say, beyond the generalities
of an adequate theology of grace, is that regular contact with the living
God transforms human nature. Redemption is not simply being
grabbed back from the edge of hellfire. More intrinsically, it is being
opened to forces of re-creation. Grace is healing and elevating at the
same time. It is healing because it is elevating.

     When people open themselves to God, through God's prior work-
ing in their hearts, they experience the cleansing, repair, nourishment,
and movement to new planes of vision, being, and love that they require, if original sin, as a symbol of everything wrong, is to shrink,
toward the day when it might be no more. Specifically, in the love that
people embraced by God feel poured into their hearts by the Holy
Spirit, everything that seemed impossible (peace, justice, joy, creativity)
becomes possible. Then one beholds that God makes all things new.
Then one believes that there are no dead ends.

     Nothing is impossible with God, because God is by definition possi-
bility—creative love. The only practical problem is how to gain union
with God such that the transformations of grace are not merely occa-
sional. The only conceptual problem is why sin should seem so strong
and grace so fragile. But perhaps these are not real problems. Perhaps
God is accomplishing what we need and cry out for even though we
cannot feel or realize it. At Easter, when we meet the risen Christ, that
"perhaps" fades away. At Easter, Christian faith finds it certain that

God has defeated evil once and for all time, for all people. Would that Lao Tzu might encounter Easter—it would be fascinating to watch the ripples and see the changes in his political philosophy.

Shinto Spirituality

Buddhism, Confucianism, and Taoism all made significant impacts on traditional Japanese culture. The native outlook with which they interacted, Shinto, was flexible enough to accommodate such new ideas as the Buddhist view of karma and the Confucian notion of filial piety. Taoism, close to nature, provided much of the vocabulary for translating Buddhist views into Chinese terms. Shinto, also close to nature, was most akin to Taoism, though it also expressed such ancient Japanese ideas as purity and blood relations.

The great imperial Shrine at Ise, which dates to early in the first century of the Christian era, has remained a place of pilgrimage where Japanese might renovate their spirits by encountering a pristine Shinto setting. The monk who wrote the following account of his visit to Ise thought in Buddhist as well as Shinto categories, but the bulk of his description in this section is Shinto: "When on the way to this Shrine one does not feel like an ordinary person any longer but as though reborn in another world. How solemn is the unearthly shadow of the huge groves of ancient pines and chamaecyparis, and there is a delicate pathos in the few rare flowers that have withstood the winter frosts so gaily. The cross-beams of the Torii or Shinto gate way is without any curve, symbolizing by its straightness the sincerity of the direct beam of the Divine promise. The shrine-fence is not painted red nor is the Shrine itself roofed with cedar shingles. The eaves, with their rough reed-thatch, recall memories of the ancient days when the roofs were not trimmed. So did they spare expense out of compassion for the hardships of the people."[8]

The Shinto deities, known as the *kami*, traditionally number 800,000. In effect they are the geniuses or resident spirits suggested by anything striking, whether in the landscape or in human affairs. Striking things in the landscape predominate, however, and Ise is primarily a lovely grove of trees and streams, with a few shrine buildings housing regalia representing the kami. The pilgrim writing this account is sensitive to the natural beauty of Ise, and he lets it work on his spirit, to induce a mood of reverence and renewal. One of the main themes working through Shinto symbolism is of purification or renewal. Ise is by the sea, and the salt used in Shinto rituals suggests the constant renewal of sea-waters. The shrines at Ise are torn down regularly, to be rebuilt and make a fresh start. Shinto stays close enough to the processes of change we noted in Chuang Tzu to offer a message of hope: things do turn over, there can be fresh starts.

For Christians, the connection between aesthetics and religion makes Shinto an interesting study. One cannot separate the two in native Japanese spirituality. The majesty and delicacy of nature are the prime symbols of the Shinto deity. Buddhist schools that flourished in Japan, such as Zen, put a sharper focus on this symbolism. The fall of a cherry blossom might trigger enlightenment. The serenity of a rock garden called to mind emptiness, a prime Mahayana symbol for ultimate reality. In native Japanese thought, nature was more perfect than humanity. Trees and animals do what they have to do, express their natures, without the fuss and internal division that afflict human beings. Indeed, enlightened human beings become more natural, overcoming the dualities of their psychology and living holistically. Frequently, beauty is both the path to wholeness and its expression. For example, painting with "no mind," master calligraphers express themselves effortlessly.

Hans Urs von Balthasar is the Catholic theologian who has paid most attention to beauty, reminding us that it is a prime attribute of God. By doing this, he has rescued aesthetics from the forecourts, if not the backwaters, of spirituality, placing them at the center. The God we worship when we follow Christ is beautiful. Such beauty is not separate from the divine power, goodness, love, or other attributes, but neither is it inferior. There is a splendor to God, and those with whom God communes experience it. The nimbus surrounding a saint in traditional Christian iconography represents an effulgence of the divine splendor. The saints often shone with light after their encounters with God. On the model of the transfiguration of Jesus (Mt 17; Mk 9), they translated heavenly experience into a bodily glow. And the Christian sacraments can be beautiful in their very simplicity. As people break the solid bread, drink the ruby wine, feel the oil of anointing balm their foreheads, they can realize that every decent thing in creation has a beauty, an integrity, that reflects its mysterious source.

Nowadays any reflection bearing on nature is bound to raise the matter of ecological destruction, and any Christian theology of nature has to deal with the practical question of how to convert the west, if not the whole world, from its pernicious views of the earth. One important key is natural beauty. If Christian theologians can overcome the denigration of natural beauty that sprang up frequently in the past, they can repair some of the damage to the western psyche responsible for much ravaging of nature.

Natural beauty is not something indifferent, let alone a threat to pure Christian faith. The biblical polemic against the fertility religions of Israel's neighbors need not mean that natural beauty is a trap. Certainly, the biblical God transcends nature, and the biblical writers were wise to recognize the distortions that fertility religions could introduce when they overemphasized sex. But the serenity of nature is a powerful image of God, who takes sabbaths even though working always. And the beauty of the mountains, the seas, the forests, the rivers, the animals sings about the beauty of their creator. The human spirit needs the space of a healthy nature, an unsettled and undamaged wilderness, to soar to its creator. Just as the ancient cathedrals reached up toward heaven and made the human spirit feel properly small, so a healthy nature reminds men and women of the true scale of things.

The spirituality inculcated by Shinto did not foster devotion to a personal God. When fused with devotional Buddhism, it could venerate Buddhist saints as indistinguishable from kami, but throughout its history its main reference remained the natural world. Traditional Japanese defined their distinctiveness in terms of the beauty of their native habitat. The Shinto mythology has creation center in the Japanese islands, and throughout Japanese cultural history a sense of gratitude and pride for the beauty of those islands has played a strong part in clan and national identity. Early Christian missionaries might take issue with the practice of venerating spirits of local places, but nowadays we can interpret such practices as praiseworthy efforts to honor the mystery of being and beauty. Such efforts are in line with the worldwide practice of venerating emblems of being, fertility, and beauty.

Missionaries might have considered this to be polytheism, and so to be repugnant in view of the biblical teachings about the oneness of God, but nowadays one can ask further questions. Might it not be that such practices express, in less differentiated language, the Christian instinct that God is present everywhere, sustaining all things in being? Is it actually true that those worshiping before stone altars or bowing to striking trees think them independent deities, or are they simply trying to express their soul-deep reverence for the Force responsible for all the good things in existence? Shinto is a good tradition to study, because originally it generated little ideology. The aesthetic component was high, but the philosophical component was low. Using a language of beauty, then, Christians wanting to understand "polytheists" might break through many traditional barriers, realizing that their one God has long been willing to be reverenced in many different places and moods.

Shinto as a Political Ideology

Shinto has a bad name in western memories, because it is associated with the chauvinism of the Japanese people that helped to precipitate World War II. The idea had arisen that the Japanese people were select in the eyes of divinity, and that their emperor was divine. This was repugnant to western ears, because of western monotheism or secularism, but more because it seemed to lie at the roots of Japanese self-aggrandizement and aggression. While the conception and role of the emperor continue to be a freighted subject in contemporary Japan, on the whole the Japanese have accepted the terms forced on them by the Allies who defeated them in World War II. Thus Shinto is not now the focus of nationalistic or ethnic solidarity that it was in the 1930s and 1940s.

We may gather how such solidarity worked out in practice from some of the terms of the Act by which the Allies disestablished Shinto in 1945: "In order to free the Japanese people from direct or indirect compulsion to believe or profess to believe in a religion or cult officially designated by the state, and in order to lift from the Japanese people the burden of compulsory financial support of an ideology which has contributed to their war guilt, defeat, suffering, privation, and present deplorable condition, and in order to prevent the recurrence of the perversion of Shinto theory and beliefs into militaristic and ultra-nationalistic propaganda designed to delude the Japanese people and lead them into wars of aggression, all financial support from public funds and all official affiliation with Shinto and Shinto shrines are prohibited and will cease immediately . . . [and Japan will reject (1)] The doctrine that the Emperor of Japan is superior to the heads of other

states because of ancestry, descent, or special origin. (2) The doctrine
that the people of Japan are superior to the people of other lands
because of ancestry, descent, or special origin. (3) The doctrine that the
islands of Japan are superior to other lands because of divine or special
origin. (4) Any other doctrine which tends to delude the Japanese people into embarking upon wars of aggression or to glorify the use of force
as an instrument for the settlement of disputes with other people."[9]

Though western interests and prejudices lie behind this document
forced upon the Japanese, it suggests the proportions to which Shinto
mythology had grown by the dawn of World War II. Japanese people-
hood, long a favorite theme, had become an eastern version of "manifest destiny." Just as Hitler had convinced the Germans that they had
inalienable rights to territory and leadership in Europe, so Japanese
leaders had urged their people to assume their lofty, divinely given
place in the sun. The Allies wanted to devastate this arrogance, reduc-
ing Shinto to the status of merely another religious option for the
Japanese, who henceforth would live in a secular state that established
no religion as privileged.

Historians and sociologists can continue to debate the extent to
which the Allies succeeded. Certainly contemporary Japan is a more
secular country than was true two generations ago, but how much
Japanese ethnicity has simply gone underground, or translated itself
into a rationale for economic domination, is difficult to assess. What the
Christian theologian interested in a global spirituality is bound to note
is the theme of election. By the time that the Japanese attacked Pearl
Harbor, they had a myth that made them unique among the nations of
the earth. How greatly does this myth differ from that of Jews, who have
thought themselves uniquely covenanted to God, or that of Christians,
who have thought that Christ was the only way to salvation, or that of
Muslims, who have regarded the Qur'an as the final revelation of God?
The answer sometimes seems to be: Not very much. Indeed, at the
times when Jews, Christians, or Muslims have strode off to battle thinking themselves commissioned to conduct holy war on God's behalf, the
difference has been imperceptible.

One of the obvious requirements for peace in the twenty-first
century is a rejection of all such arrogance. At the present, fundamentalist Muslims seem to be the worst offenders, but in many Jewish,
Christian, and other hearts lies a conviction that "we" are special,

uniquely loved by God. That cannot be so. No valid theology of revelation can set one people apart so that, simply by being Jews, Christians, Muslims, or anything else, they have a special standing before God. No notion of a "covenant" between God and a given people can make them elect, in the sense of loved by God preferentially apart from any merits of their own.

In saying this, we are offering a theological opinion, not something that we can guarantee from scripture or tradition. Many people, east and west, have indulged the fantasy that theirs was the land where creation arose, or that they were the first truly human beings, or that their God was unique and made them first among all the nations of the world. That seems to us pure self-service, and so one of the many things that has to go if people (as groups or individuals) are to mature before God. In the Christian case, this means a distinction between what Christians think that Christ has accomplished and what they think that Christ's accomplishment implies for their own dignity.

Christians have to think that Christ is God's definitive revelation —the self-disclosure and self-gift that gives history its eschatological (once-and-for-all) meaning. That is what calling Christ divine, the savior, the resurrected one, or the Lord implies. On the other hand, Christians do not have to think, should not think, that faith in Christ makes them better than other human beings. Faith in Christ opens them to the benefits of salvation and divinization. It is the way that what they find to be the clearest indication of God's purposes, the fullest gift of God's love, comes to men and women. But other people receive or accomplish the essence of Christian faith, either through simply following their consciences or through living out the cultural and religious traditions that they have inherited.

Specifically, Jews, Muslims, Hindus, Buddhists, and all other religionists can come into the salvation and divinization that Christians find in Christ without becoming Christians. There is no strict tie between explicit membership in the community of Christ's disciples (the church) and finding the love of God that brings salvation. Christians must believe that their faith, theology, sacramental system, social forms, and the like square best with the definitive revelation of the divine love that they revere in Jesus of Nazareth, but they cannot think that their forms, so limited by human weaknesses and conditioned by historical circumstances, exhaust God's ways of bringing people to salvation. Indeed, they cannot think that they have any privileged status, simply because they belong to the organization or history that Christ stimulated.

It is a central Christian conviction that no person knows with certitude whether he or she is saved. It is equally central to Christian faith that all salvation is a work of God, who remains sovereignly free. So, without relinquishing a bit of their admiration of Christ or their dedication to Christ, Christians have to reject all chauvinism. Even when they have done their very best, even when they have become saints, they remain unprofitable servants.

The ecumenical advantage of embracing such a Christian humility is that, when sincere, it gives Christians grounds for urging Jews, Muslims, Japanese, and all other people to put aside their arrogant claims to uniqueness or special standing before God and join common humanity—all their sisters and brothers, who are equally images of God, apples of God's eye. Since such arrogant claims still contribute to wars, genocides, and immense suffering, removing them is nothing merely academic. In the Middle East, for example, it is a condition for survival. Until Jews, Muslims, and Christians in Israel, Lebanon, and other countries relinquish their (originally religiously based) pride and arrogance, they will continue to slaughter one another, and so to offend their God. Until Hindus and Muslims in India effect a similar relinquishment, they will continue to defile both themselves and their religious traditions. So the issue raised by Shinto chauvinism is far from being a dead letter. It remains with us in all too virulent form, awaiting a global spirituality persuasive enough to bring all people to their knees confessing their distance from the holiness of God and so their common humanity.

NOTES

1. *Analects*, 3:12–13, in THE ANALECTS OF CONFUCIUS, trans. Arthur Waley (New York: Vintage Books, n.d. [orig. 1938]), p. 97.

2. *Tahsueh, Liki*, 42:8, in THE WISDOM OF CONFUCIUS, ed. Lin Yutang (New York: Random House, 1938), pp. 148–149.

3. Chu Hsi, "A Treatise on *Jen*," in A SOURCE BOOK IN CHINESE PHILOSOPHY, ed. Wing-tsit Chan (Princeton: Princeton University Press, 1963), pp. 593–594.

4. *Tao Te Ching,* 5, in ibid., p. 141.

5. *Chuang Tzu,* 6, in CHUANG TZU: BASIC WRITINGS, trans. Burton Watson (New York: Columbia University Press, 1964), pp. 80–81.

6. John Casey, SPARTINA (New York: Alfred A. Knopf, 1989), p. 371.

7. *Tao Te Ching,* 31, in A SOURCEBOOK IN CHINESE PHILOSOPHY, p. 155.

8. A. L. Sadler, THE ISE DAIJINGU SANKEIKI OR DIARY OF A PILGRIM TO ISE (Tokyo: Meiji Japan Society, 1940), as reprinted in RELIGION IN THE JAPANESE EXPERIENCE: SOURCES AND INTERPRETATIONS, ed. H. Byron Earhart (Belmont: Dickenson [Wadsworth], 1974), pp. 25–26.

9. D. C. Holtom, MODERN JAPAN AND SHINTO NATIONALISM (New York: Paragon, 1963), as reprinted in ibid., pp. 29, 31.

Chapter 5

Judaism and Islam

Psalm 1

The hallmark of Jewish spirituality is reverence for Torah. Torah is divine instruction (revelation, guidance, law). Narrowly, it is the teaching that God gave to Moses on Mount Sinai. Broadly, it is everything in scripture and tradition that points out the way that God's people ought to walk, if they are to fulfill the covenant. In postbiblical times, the interpretation of Torah has entailed a mastery of the Talmud, a collection of prior interpretations of key points by eminent rabbis.

Nonetheless, the centrality of meditating on Torah is as old as the Psalms, the basic prayer-book of ancient Israel. Indeed, at the beginning of the book of Psalms, functioning like an overture, is a reflection (begging to be prayed) that equates blessedness (standing approved by God) with delighting in Torah: "Blessed is the man [person] who walks not in the counsel of the wicked, nor stands in the way of sinners, nor sits in the seat of scoffers, but his delight is in the law of the Lord, and on his law he meditates day and night. He is like a tree planted by streams of water, that yields its fruit in its season, and its leaf does not wither. In all that he does, he prospers" (Ps 1:1–3, RSV).

The counsel of God, expressed in Torah, is the opposite of the counsel of the wicked and its foe. The way of sinners, the seat of scoffers—they represent the alternative to a life directed by Torah. For the just person, blessed by God, Torah is a delight. It gives light to the mind, warmth to the heart, hope to the deepest spirit. So the blessed meditate on Torah day and night. They take it to heart, let it seep into their marrow. It becomes the language that trips from their tongue when they try to describe reality, especially in its ethical aspects. It serves up a stream of images to direct their desires so that they may

106

please God. Without meditation on Torah, Psalm 1 suggests, the joy would leak away from the souls of the blessed. The light would dim and their hopes would grow cold. So the blessed find nourishment and security in Torah. Torah roots them in the source of human fruitfulness: the goodness of God.

The prosperity that Psalm 1 promises will flow from meditating on Torah is material as well as spiritual. Seldom does the Hebrew Bible separate the two. The most central theology of the covenant, that developed by the Deuteronomistic school, considered prosperity the rightful reward for fidelity. In contrast, infidelity would bring disaster. By the time of the book of Job this theology had come into crisis, because it seemed apparent that the just could suffer as badly as the wicked. Indeed, it seemed apparent that the wicked could prosper. Where, then, was the oversight, the providence, of God?

The easy way to redeem Psalm 1 from the deficiencies of the Deuteronomistic school is to make "prosperity" religious. Second Isaiah interpreted the experience of exile in deep terms, coming to think that God would draw good from Israel's sufferings. Suffering itself could become the occasion to learn new things about the justice and goodness of God. Christianity used the Servant Songs of Second Isaiah to interpret the fate of Jesus. Innocent, he had suffered and died so that others might prosper. His fate took human understanding of God's ways to a new depth, where it became credible that God suffers with those who keep faith, holding their fates in the palm of his hand.

So the law that has preoccupied most Jews and many Christians has been rich and many-leveled. Meditating on Torah, and trying to live by the precepts of Torah, has been far from legalistic. Without a grasp of the inner pulse of Torah, one could not interpret it well. Such a grasp came only from long, heartfelt study. The surest way to attain it was to put oneself at the feet of wise elders and swim in the stream of traditional interpretation. Thus studying Torah became the most honored occupation. When traditional Jews thought about life at its best, time for studying Torah, and freedom in which to fulfill the demands of Torah, stood out. This ideal applied only to men, but women had a parallel dream: to run a household rich in the blessings of Torah— observance, goodness, joy in the favor of God.

Christian attitudes about law are more ambivalent. Inasmuch as the followers of Jesus found contemporary interpretations of Torah stifling, they pictured Jesus as a great champion of spiritual freedom. In saying that the sabbath was made for human beings, and not human beings for the sabbath, the evangelical Christ put forward a radical interpretation. Inasmuch as assumptions rooted in traditional interpretations of Torah caused Jesus' enemies to reject him (he could not be the messiah, let alone the Son of God, because he did not meet his enemies' criteria [it is doubtful that anyone could]), the followers of Jesus were tempted to curl their lip.

And yet, we know that they did not. For the first two generations, Torah continued to be important to many Christians who still thought of themselves as Jews. Only with the admission of many Gentiles into the Christian community did Torah become a matter of crisis, and even then Christian decisions created a "new" covenant, with its "new" instruction or law. The gospel of Matthew is the clearest of the four on the matter of retaining the sanctity of the Torah. The epistles of Paul, which wrestle endlessly with the place of the Torah in Christian life, seem to oppose the gospel to the Torah, but in fact the matter is more complicated.

What does emerge in the history of Christian spirituality, though, is a different sense of obligation. Christians have not tied their identity to any code as closely as Jews have tied their identity to Torah (which of course has always been much more than a code). Christians have tied their identity to Christ, when they knew their faith, making him the summary of God's instruction. The Spirit given by Christ to be the advocate for his followers before God has seemed more interior and supple than any code, biblical or canonical, could ever be. And where the Spirit moved, there was liberty—not to the despising of good order, but to the suspicion that no set of letters could ever render God's will fully adequately.

This is not to say that the Christian churches, the Roman Catholic prominent among them, have not become legalistic. Experience suggested that few people could follow only the interior guidance of the Spirit without getting into trouble. Most people needed the counsel of wise elders, the guidance of past tradition, and the easiest way to present these was to fashion laws or rules. When bureaucracies arose to formulate and enforce such rules, Christians were back to many of their old problems with the Pharisees.

For the best appreciation of traditional Judaism, Christians have to develop positive understandings of Torah. It is Torah as a matter of delight, food for the soul, that will bring the long-standing Jewish devotion to religious study into focus. One analogue from Christian tradition is what many medievals called *lectio divina*. This is the use of instructional materials for spiritual nourishment more than intellectual or academic insight. *Lectio divina* does not imply that we should be ignorant about the Bible or the Talmud or any other authoritative texts we use, but it does imply that our first interest is letting them lighten our burdens, restore our courage, nourish us again with the goodness of God.

What we learn when we use traditional materials in this way is the priority of their divine source. The Spirit of God can suggest so many rich possibilities in a venerable text (for example, Psalm 1) that we soon find ourselves turning from rumination about the key images to praise of God. In other words, we soon find ourselves praying—seeking God heart to heart. Whether we've memorized the text or not, whether we know how the authorities line up about it, becomes secondary. The text has come alive as a font of revelation, as it presumably was for those who first gave it form, and so Torah, divine instruction, has become immediate and personal—a stream of water ensuring that we shall not wither.

Mysticism

The roots of Jewish mysticism, as well as Jewish study of Torah, lie in the Bible. If there is a single image that attracted Jews who wanted to know God intimately, in spiritual flights, it is the chariot vision recorded in Ezekiel 1. This vision is too long for us to quote in full. The four living creatures whom the prophet beholds stand for the heavenly entourage. At the center, though, is an intimation of divinity itself, which is like fire: "In the midst of the living creatures there was something that looked like burning coals of fire, like torches moving to and fro among the living creatures; and the fire was bright, and out of the fire went forth lightning" (1:13). The Cabbalists, those Jewish mystics of the medieval period who loved to ponder imagery from scripture, were the foremost students of Ezekiel's figures, but in fact all schools of Jewish mysticism regarded the chariot vision as the supreme symbolism for divinity.

Christian mysticism did not place so great an emphasis on the chariot. More to the liking of the classical Christian mystics was the romance depicted in the Song of Songs. The rabbis did not neglect the Song of Songs, and the Christian masters commented on the chariot, but instinctively they struck different emphases. This is an interesting difference, so perhaps it will profit us to reflect on it.

The pride of Jewish theology is monotheism. The purity of the one God amazes the traditional Jewish theologian. And from such monotheism comes a strong aversion to idolatry, even to any representation of God. Judaism, like Islam, prefers an aniconic approach to spirituality. The safest way to think about God is to refuse to depict the divine nature. Yet, curiously, Jewish mysticism does not stress unknowing as Christian mysticism does. It is not lured by images of darkness, obnubilation, or the mind's shutting down. For Christian mystics the loss of the beloved depicted in the Song of Songs is like the spirit's sense that God has departed—slipped away in the night. Christian mystics have also stressed the hiddenness of God, who would only show Moses his hind parts. Some scholars think that Neoplatonic philosophy shifted Christian spirituality in the direction of darkness, and it is clear that Pseudo-Dionysius, a great influence, owed much to Greek thought. But more crucial seems to have been the actual experience of contemplation. When they sought to know and love God, the great Christian saints, from the desert fathers on, soon realized that they had to submit to a process of purification that would strip their minds as well as their wills.

The rabbis seem to have been more insistent on holding onto their minds. Whether from their constant study of Torah, or from their love of the divine speech, they seldom made silence or unknowing or darkness their preferred imagery. So the figures from Ezekiel 1, so striking or even bizarre, came to stand for the dangerous but still attractive knowledge of God that might come in mystical moments. Imagery remained central, even though monotheistic theology was a caution against imagery. The goodness of creation, which kept the rabbis from the celibacy that most Christian masters embraced, and the power of the studious mind, which finally had to do business through images (words), militated against a plunge into imageless, apophatic prayer. Thus the *Zohar,* perhaps the most influential Cabbalistic text, is full of imaginative plays with scriptural figures.

What the deepest Christian masters realized, of course, is that even darkness is an image. Indeed, they realized that even feelings are no guarantee when it comes to interpreting the special overtures through which divinity makes its presence felt experientially. If we take the scholastic definition of mysticism, which makes it "undergoing divine influence," then mysticism proper is passive. It follows that one cannot determine what happens in mystical encounters, or even whether they will occur. Mysticism in the strict sense is completely God's doing. Certainly God tends to touch people who have purified themselves, but if divinity wishes it can raise up mystics from ordinary stones. Still, it is useful to record what God has done in favoring some with mysticism in a strict sense, because God's doings, as always, reveal the divine goodness.

What God has done for those favored with mysticism in a strict sense is make the divine mystery and priority experiential. Beyond theological concepts, however orthodox and helpful, the God experienced by the mystics has taught them what it means to be a creature, a sinner, and yet one loved by God more fully than they could ever imagine. Indeed, God has taught them that divinization, the process through which God takes people into the life of Father, Son, and Spirit, is a love affair. At each stage of consolation, the message is that God is more intimate, more loving, than human beings could hope. At each stage of desolation, discouragement, apparent abandonment, the message is that God is so pure that human beings have to learn how apparent absence is God's stable presence.

Is it possible to live beyond not just imagination but also feeling? How can one navigate, when the night is so dark, or the sea is so immense, that neither up nor down, neither forward nor back, is clear? Can one trust that desire, longing for God, is already a profitable prayer, or is it also necessary to sense the divine presence or be able to focus on it? These questions may not interest the casual student of Christianity, but they are burning issues for those who have tasted the goodness of the Lord sufficiently to know that no other sweetness can compare.

The chariot that Ezekiel saw depended on the regalia of ancient Near Eastern royalty. The Lord was a king, and so it was fitting that he be attended by a splendid retinue, that he travel in a handsome chariot. But the human analogies broke down. He was more like fire than any human king suggested. His holiness was such that only flames could represent it. And he moved as he wished: forward, back, quick as thought, brilliant as lightning. For he was primary, and any natural phenomena were secondary. They derived from him, not he from them. Ezekiel was interested in the divine purity because Ezekiel was a priest, convinced that the exile in which Judah found itself was a condign punishment for its flouting of Torah. Torah was the way that Judah might be holy as its holy Lord required. His vision convinced Ezekiel that Judah could never be holy as its Lord required—unless its Lord made it holy. In the vision of the dry bones gaining flesh and coming to life (Ez 37), the prophet learned that the Spirit of God could do what human beings could not. He learned that resurrection is possible, and that therefore his people might emerge from their exile restored by God's mercy.

Christian mystics have learned the same lesson, which they have tended to interpret by reference to the resurrection of Christ. No matter how dark their sense of exile or distance from God, they could hope that God would bring them light like that shining from the resurrected Christ. If Christ had descended to the depths, to free the souls of the dead, certainly they could descend to the depths of creaturehood, realizing how they were, quite literally, nothing without the divine word, touch, or breath. If they died to sin, they could live in grace, and this living in grace made them long to die physically—to complete their course, which was a trial and pilgrimage, and be united with their beloved.

So Christian mystics tended to understand the symbolism of the Song of Songs individually, likening the losses and gains of the lovers to trysts with God and separations. Jewish exegetes tended to stress the fate of Israel, the Jewish community, which now seemed to enjoy God's favor and then seemed to lose it. Either way, the interesting thing is the greater interest of Christians, whose theology made a greater place for iconography, because of the incarnation, in the darkness, the nonrepresentative character of God and mystical experience. Perhaps that is due to the Christian sense that, when meeting God, believers stand in the "position" of the Son, facing the Father who is endless origination— light so bright, immensity so vast, that the creature is bound to experience it as darkness.

Finding God

Neither the study of Torah nor mystical experience took pious Jews away from the world, in the sense of absolving them of the need to sanctify all aspects of daily life. In fact, the concern of the Torah with all the minutiae of daily life was precisely an effort to hallow everything, from sleeping to rising, from eating to defecation. Something of this spirit of hallowing comes through in the following lovely midrash: "How does a man find his Father who is in heaven? He finds him by good deeds, and study of the Torah. And the Holy One, blessed be he, finds man through love, through brotherhood, through respect, through companionship, through truth, through peace, through bending the knee, through humility, through studious session, through commerce lessened, through the service of the masters, through the discussion of students, through a good heart, through decency, through No that is really No, through Yes that is really Yes."[1]

First, it is interesting that though human beings have two ways of finding God, good deeds and studying Torah, God has numerous ways of finding human beings. If we were to diagram these relations, the line of ascent to God would be sharp, while the line of descent by God would be pitched gently, becoming almost horizontal. The suggestion would be that God meets us in every decent preoccupation. Whenever human beings are humane, God is in their midst. How hopeful a theology! The rabbis responsible for such a conviction knew daily life to be full of potential meetings with God. Living in bustling families, having to earn a living, loving the friends with whom they discussed the Torah, these holy men realized that everything could be graced.

Second, the end of this small quotation is intriguing, reminiscent of Jesus' advice to let our speech be yea, yea and nay, nay (Mt 5:37). Judaism has been an articulate religion. Living by the word (more powerful in desert cultures than the vision), it has talked and talked, written and written, studied and studied. In this text the potential for weariness with so much speech seems to shine through. A no that is really a no is plain speech, coming from a pure heart. A yes that is really a yes is a word to rely on, a word that creates friendship. All of us bend words to our impure purposes so often that all of us can appreciate the value of a straight no or a straight yes. All of us realize that we bastardize the gifts of speech and thought that make us images of God, so all of us can admire a conception that is thoroughly legitimate.

For our interest in social justice, plain, legitimate speech is riveting. Social justice, which has ranked high on the agenda of traditional Judaism, depends above all on a fundamental honesty. When people tell one another the truth, and act as they promise, they have good social relations. Their buying and selling, explaining and receiving, being helped and giving help back in return proceed with few difficulties. The rabbis knew this, and they wanted their knowledge to bear fruit in happy households, peaceful communities. So they tried to help men make their word their bond, to help women make their words helpful and welcoming. For all human words lived within the overarching word of the Torah, God's yes and no to human beings. God's yes, the stupendous favor of the covenant, founded all human agreement and affection. God's no, the favor of indicating what misdeeds constituted the path of death, allowed the community to keep itself clean, faithful, true to its core identity. So all human words, whether affirmative or negative, had a holy paradigm to live up to. When people spoke in awareness that their Lord had spoken wonderfully to them, they created a spirituality of truth and fellowship.

Christians have their own sense of the divine Word, of course, and some of the New Testament writers said explicitly that Christ represents God's yes to humankind (for example, 2 Cor 2:19–20). Christians also have their own sense of how God comes to people through ordinary experiences, though the ascetical strain of Christianity, which has meant that many masters lived apart from ordinary, family life, sometimes blunted this sense. Trying to resharpen it, Wendy Wright has recently developed a spirituality of family life. In a chapter devoted to suggesting how ordinary times can make us wonder at God's presence, she shows that even the smallest member of the family can become alert, a watcher for God's advent: "My sense of the meeting [of her family, in Advent] is that we are ready to sing 'O Come, O Come Emmanuel' and get on with our evening. But it seems unfair not to include her [the three year old, who has been playing with the candle wax] in the reflections. Not really expecting an answer, I turn to her and ask, 'What do *you* think we should do to make our family a more peaceful place?' She pauses in her wax-rolling and looks up at us. Slowly she folds both hands in front of her and looks solemnly from face to face. 'Watch for God,' she answers."[2]

The rabbis would agree. If we watch for God, we are likely to spy out some of God's comings, some of the divine presence in our midst. We are likely to realize that the cup of cold water given thoughtfully, the promise kept, the visit to the sick person, the money made over to the poor, and all the other gestures of solidarity, small and great, are visitations from God. The dwelling of God is with human beings, for God's own inscrutable reasons and purposes. To our amazement, we have to confess that scripture makes God a lover of human beings, a frequenter of our so often dusty byways.

The gospel of John has the Word pitch its tent in our midst. The epistle to the Philippians says that Christ did not cling to his heavenly privileges but emptied himself, becoming our servant. These are brave, astounding words, but how do they work out in practice? What could they possibly mean, two thousand years after the death and resurrection that were supposed to be the definitive victory? They could mean that the definitive victory is a matter of radical possibility rather than tidy accomplishment—that it is enough to think that God's word to us is a yes that enables us to say yes to one another. And the pledges of God to be with us could work out just as God promised they would, when he gave Moses his name—the no-name that guaranteed only that he would be with Israel as he wished, sojourning with it through time (Ex 3:14).

The work of social justice, in small matters or large, is a presence of God. The rightness that social justice insinuates is part of God's sojourn. Especially when they do the right thing at cost, people realize that they are choosing the light. They could choose the darkness. They could bend the truth, the better impulse, and seize a quicker profit. But they sense that to bend the truth, or hold back the help they felt stirred to offer, would be to deflect the presence of God. God is there directly, when people speak a yes that is a real yes, or a no that is a real no. God is still there, when people lie or cheat, but only indirectly, in the pain that such a distortion of the human spirit creates.

The Christian realignment of these humane perceptions is that all truth reflects the Logos, who is the wholly truthful Word of God. When the Father expresses himself, the full truth of who he is stands forth, though not apart from him, in the Son. The Son is the self-knowledge of the Father, as the Spirit is the love that the truths of the Father and the Son breathe forth. So the Son, come into our history, become a partaker of our flesh, has a special stake in truth and light, a special animus against lies and spiritual darkness. The Son has a special stake in social justice, being intimated whenever and wherever men and women do for one another what is right. If we watch for God, we shall see many advents in the holy spaces created when we do what is right.

Wisdom and Justice

We tend to associate wisdom with prayer and study. The wise person sees things as they truly are, and things as they truly are stand under the aspect of eternity. Only when our horizon stretches toward God can we estimate any creature wisely. For Judaism, wisdom naturally devolved from penetration of the Torah. It was by immersing themselves in the thought-world of God's law that the rabbis hoped to become fully realistic, and so holy as their Lord was holy.

Yet the prophetic tradition that the rabbis inherited, and their stable residence in family life, kept this notion of wisdom from becoming either esoteric or elitist. The wisdom that the Jewish community needed most could not be separated from good deeds. The practice of faith always remained more important than the theory. What women did as dedicated wives, mothers, and supports of the community more than balanced what men did by studying. That did not mean that women received the honors that learned men did, but it did mean that many rabbis realized that their learning was worth little unless it animated holy, happy living.

We find this conviction in the following sayings attributed to Rabbi Hanina ben Dosa: "R. Hanina ben Dosa said: Everyone whose fear of sin comes before his wisdom his wisdom endures; and everyone whose wisdom comes before his fear of sin his wisdom does not endure. . . . He [also] used to say: Everyone whose deeds are more than his wisdom, his wisdom endures. And everyone whose wisdom is more than his deeds, his wisdom does not endure."[3]

When our deeds are more than our wisdom, we are proving that we do better than we know, that we love more than we understand, that our heart is purer than our brain. For prophetic religions such as Judaism, Christianity, and Islam, the whole is more significant than the part. Acts, deeds, are the language of the whole. Thoughts, words, are the language of the part, the frail understanding. Certainly the heart depends on the head. The more clearly we see, the better we are likely to love and act. But the mystery in which we are immersed defeats our seeing, our knowing, almost before we begin. On the other hand, it yields to our loving, because it is a whole wanting to embrace the whole of us. The horizon of God that makes us wise is an infinite mystery soliciting our love.

The Christian sense of the relations between knowing and loving, wisdom and holiness, is the same as the Jewish. The priority lies with the whole and the heart. Indeed, for both religions the heart, what we love, colors what we know, our wisdom, significantly. Love of neighbor, like prayer, is a *schola affectus*. Both tutor our sensibility. Both shape us, through the years, to a depth and simplicity that confute worldly notions of wisdom. So the most revered masters, in both Christianity and Judaism, have been childlike. No matter how learned or gifted, they have shone with a winsome, an almost playful, simplicity. One thinks of the Baal Shem Tov and Saint Francis of Assisi. One thinks of Pope John XXIII. These are masters whose example means more than their words. These are masters so full of joy that immediately one wants to become their apprentice. The Baal Shem Tov has taught a dozen generations of Hasidim that true service of God requires singing and dancing. Nothing less can convey the fullness of the love that God gives. Saint Francis has made poverty romantic—the eager lightness of being that the knight requires if he is to serve his lovely lady. And Pope John XXIII has kept a glow in many Christian hearts, even when the fire that he started by convening the Second Vatican Council has seemed to flicker. If the pope could laugh and not take himself seriously, the rest of the church could not be in terrible shape. For by laughing and not taking himself seriously, John XXIII reminded everyone that the church, like the whole world, rests in the hands of God—the best custody imaginable.

Rabbi Hanina ben Dosa was impressed by the fear of sin. If a person appreciated the holiness of God, knowing that the beginning of wisdom is fear of the Lord, he or she was not likely to offend God, or to grow complacent. Complacency in the spiritual life is pride—focusing on one's accomplishments rather than one's deficiencies. Admittedly a wrongful focus on our deficiencies can discourage us. The better focus is reflective: what we see when we make God our mirror. God is perfect, without defect. In contrast, we are shot through with imperfection. But God chooses to make us acceptable. If we will allow it, God will wash what is dirty, iron out what is wrinkled, heal what has been festering. This will not make us perfect, but it will make us better images of God, and so better helps to our neighbors.

The wisdom that we generate through our prayer and study, our experience and reflection, is always much less than our dependence on God. Indeed, the wisdom that we generate boils down to appreciating how totally we depend on God. The simplicity and joy that characterized the Baal Shem Tov, Saint Francis, John XXIII and many other especially attractive holy people were the obverse side of their understanding that they depended totally on God. They were not self-reliant, in the Pelagian sense of thinking that their salvation was a matter of their own good will. They relied completely on God, because God was their only treasure.

The wisdom that does not rely completely on God is an illusion and a trap, as we learn again and again from secular pretenders to sagacity. The best and the brightest who plot our wars, pontificate about our economies, or tell us why smart women make dumb choices are but creatures of a day, discredited before they can bring out their second editions. The art of the deal turns out to be the folly of the hubristic dealer. No doubt that is why scripture tells us not to put our trust in princes—mavens, moguls, gnomes of Zurich. The wisdom that we really need, and that we really want, cannot be hyped. The wisdom that we really need is a fear and love of God overflowing directly from experience of the divine priority.

When God is prior, we are secondary. When we are secondary, our egos do not squat on our perception. We see that time is short and eternity is long. We see that the poor are always with us, begging our help. And we see that the saints did not live for themselves. If anything, they gave themselves away imprudently, like lovers too enraptured to care about self-defense, like mothers unable not to hear the slightest cry in the night.

The Christian anchor for this line of thought, as for all lines of thought secured in wisdom, is the example of Jesus. Jesus gave himself away imprudently. Even though he knew what beat in human hearts, how much fear and self-loathing and so disorder people carried, he did not hold back. The love of his life, his Father, asked him to keep going—to the confrontations that aroused his enemies, to the revelations of new possibilities that stirred the poor, to the challenges that even his closest disciples failed. In the garden of Gethsemane Jesus had to calculate what giving himself away would finally cost him. Nearly overwhelmed, he asked his only sure support to be excused from going on. But the deepest part of him knew that, for him, by the very nature of his work for the Father, there could be no excuse, no reprieve. Having loved his own who were in the world, he had to love them to the end.

We, who seldom love even the few that we can call our own to the end, and who have contributed to the sufferings of Jesus, are wise to contemplate how Jesus ended. After the complete stripping, the full humiliation, the physical and spiritual agony, he felt consummated. There was no more love to give. He had died from love, for love, and anything more was God's doing. The resurrection was God's doing. Jesus did not raise himself. He was raised by the Father, so that all might know the righteousness of his way and the surety of his success. That is why Paul called him the wisdom and power of God. That is why Christians are bound to distrust any teaching that does not make Christ's death and resurrection, the drama of Holy Week, the inmost form of all time.

Merrymaking and Peace

"A rabbi was standing in the market place when Elijah appeared to him. The rabbi asked him, 'Is there anyone in this market place who will have a share in the World to Come?' Elijah answered that there was not. In the meantime there came two men and Elijah said, 'These will have a share in the World to Come.' The rabbi asked them, 'What is your occupation?' They answered, 'We are merrymakers; when we see men troubled in mind we cheer them up, and when we see two men quarreling we make peace between them.' "[4]

The Talmud is full of lovely stories like this. Sometimes the poet pushes aside the lawyer and the Torah breaks through ironically, amusingly. Here the irony is that so serious a question as the criteria for sharing in the world to come should receive the answer, "Make merry." The rabbi who looks about the market place is not impressed, and the prophet, harbinger of the last days when the messiah will come, agrees: mere buying and selling merit no share in heaven. But the two men in whom the prophet sees heavenly possibilities are different. Their work is non-profit, as this world sees things. They already dwell in the world to come, because they are dedicated to making peace and gladdening people's hearts.

In one imaginary scenario, these men might be "jugglers of

God"—fools sporting in harlequin garb. In another they might be
mimes, forcing the people in the market place to laugh, making them
less serious. Yet the passage associates their merrymaking with their
peacemaking—the sort of association that the rabbis poring over the
Talmud would jump on and pummel for every drop of possible meaning. Here, though, the meaning seems plain enough: there is only peace
where people have the distance, the relaxation, the self-mockery to
make merry. Peace is the sister of good humor, the fellow-traveler of
humility and joy.

When Jews read the New Testament, they can come away puz-
zled. It is not a funny book, and they are used to finding scripture funny.
True, much of the humor in the Hebrew Bible is ironic, but funny and
earthy many passages are nonetheless. From Sarah laughing at God's
promise to Samson ridiculous with Delilah, the portrayal of humanity
that we find in the Hebrew Bible has its feet on the ground, has an eye
for foibles. It is wicked that David has Uriah the Hittite, husband of
Bathsheba, killed to satisfy his lust and guilt, but it is also wicked, in the
sense of too aware of irony, that Uriah himself will not sleep with
Bathsheba because of the requirements of holy war. Uriah forces David
to reveal the full extent of his disorder, and while the Bible condemns
this, through the parable of the prophet Nathan that reveals David to
himself, it also savors the low humor that the ideal king should have
been so human as to drool over a naked (available) woman and be
unable to get her husband to sleep with her.

We don't find much of this irony, this distanced knowing about
human folly, in the New Testament. The closest we come are some of
the Johannine dialogues, such as that between Jesus and the Samaritan
woman and that between the man born blind and the Pharisees. Jesus
deals with the Samaritan woman knowingly. She has had a full sexual
history, but her grace is to accept this, realize that Jesus is a different
sort of man, and bring her previously misguided affections back to
proper focus: the holiness of God. The man born blind finally rounds
on the Pharisees and puts it to them: Has it ever been known that
someone has healed a man blind from birth; what is the point to this
endless questioning—do you want to become Jesus' disciples? The man
knows, and John delights in making us know, that blindness and sight
have become paradoxical. As a figure for faith, the blind man is the only
one who realizes what is happening. As a figure for unbelief, the Pharisees will not accredit what is right under their noses. This is all ironic, if

not funny—a satiric look at the tragic component of Jesus' history. If only those who observed him had had ordinary honesty, basic good will, things might have turned out very differently.

And yet, it is usually sober Christianity that has the most comic view of history. Judaism is hopeful, but only Christianity preaches a definitive victory in time that has settled the issue of eternity once and for all. So Christians' lagging behind Jews in ironic self-understanding, good spirits created by not taking oneself too seriously, suggests that they have not appreciated the new proportions disclosed by the resurrection.

To be sure, the resurrected Christ does not appear in the midst of the disciples cracking jokes and fingering a cigar. But the premier emotion created by Easter is joy, and this emotion would be suspect if it did not lead to some high spirits. High spirits, good spirits, wine and partying—these are images for the messianic banquet. At the consummation of history, God will throw a great party. So the eucharistic celebrations that anticipate the messianic banquet, unfolding in the traces of its projection, ought to convey at least a smidgin of festive celebration. They ought to invite into the now of history the unfettered joy at the center of the then of heaven. Now we labor, painfully, to work out our salvation, but even now the Spirit of God, God's pledge of our eventual success, can move us to wry smiles, even to full-out guffaws. Then, when history has been consummated, when wars and struggles will be no more, partying will be identical with worship. The grand chorus that the 144,000 sing has to be happy. Maybe it is rollicking.

Elijah had fled from the wicked King Ahab and the wicked Queen Jezebel. In our story, he must have been happy to be in a place, a state, where he did not have to flee any longer. In that state he would have had a keen eye for good services done to humankind. Indeed, he may have reflected that, had there been more of such good services in the olden days, he would have had more allies and not had to flee. Ahab and Jezebel took themselves seriously. A prophet mocking their bowing before new gods was no mean threat. The merrymakers come into the market place were mean threats, people easily dismissed. In their levity, they seemed insubstantial, papier-mâché compared to the solidity of buying and selling. Yet they gladdened people's hearts, so in fact they were formidable foes. Buying and selling, like idolatry, tend to take themselves seriously. Wall Street brooks little levity, nor does the Commodities Exchange. Time is money and money is serious, so time spent on making money is doubly serious. The market is not a place for playing, not a free zone where an unpredictable God may appear.

The unpredictable God that appeared in Jesus of Nazareth was like the merrymakers in wanting to lighten people's hearts and bring them peace. At the party at Cana, at the sight of Zacchaeus up in the tree, at the advent of the little children, Jesus vacated serious business and gave himself up to the moment. The moment could be for nuptial celebration, or for responding to an eagerness close to conversion, or for blessing the freshest images of God. Whatever, it asserted that God is not a grim dispenser of time, doling out heavy hours. God is free, in time as well as outside of it—free to make merry, like the Father of the prodigal son. And with this freedom, this readiness to celebrate any slightest response to his own goodness, God lures us all toward peace. Had the elder son been able to enter into the festive spirit of the father, he would not have resented the party for his younger brother's return. Had Cain been lighter, easier, in his perception of Abel, he would not have become the first murderer, forced to carry a name of infamy. Where our treasures are, there will our hearts be set. Where we take our pleasure, our recreation, our merrymaking, there will our resources for peace and justice assemble.

The Beginning of the Qur'an

The Qur'an, the heart of Islam, is a tremulous collection of revelations bequeathed through the prophet Muhammad. As they reveal the majesty of Allah, the surahs of the Qur'an attune the reader's spirit to obeisance. Just as the body bows low in Muslim prayer, so the spirit is abased. For the burning message of the Qur'an is that One only rules the world. One only is holy and Lord. That this One, this sole Holiness, is compassionate and merciful is the greatest of wonders. He who might well obliterate useless humanity has chosen to be patient and kind. The only fitting response is, "Praise Him!" The only proper result is to obey his will in all particulars and eventualities.

Muslim prayer feeds on the Qur'an. In the main, Muslims at prayer simply give back to Allah the precious verses he has sent down to them. The leitmotiv of such prayer sounds in the very first surah, which serves as the gateway to all the Qur'anic splendors: "In the name of

Allah, the compassionate, the merciful. Praise be to Allah, Lord of the Creation, the Compassionate, the Merciful, King of Judgement-day! You alone we worship, and to You alone we pray for help. Guide us to the straight path, the path of those whom You have favoured, not of those who have incurred Your wrath, nor of those who have gone astray."[5]

The deity "Allah" is cognate, linguistically, to the "El" that we meet in the Hebrew Bible. In Semitic languages, the root that they share has signified divinity. Allah is the only true deity. All others carrying the name are pretenders. Muhammad probably drew on a prior Arab monotheistic tradition, but he was remarkable among his contemporaries for denouncing the many gods and insisting that only Allah was fully real.

To speak in the name of Allah is both to position oneself solemnly, in ultimate perspective, and to claim to be the mouthpiece of God. Muslims think of Muhammad as the seal of the prophets. Before him had come many worthy spokespersons, but the prophetic words that Allah vouchsafed to him consummated divine revelation. So those words, collected into the Qur'an, have been revelation par excellence. In fact, some pious Muslims have imagined the Qur'an as eternal, existing alongside Allah in heaven. What came through Muhammad was an earthly manifestation of this eternal Qur'an, so faithful that nothing in it may be altered. It is the Word of Allah, and so the supreme authority. Any other words—law codes, poems, theologies—are miserably inferior. Unless they cede to the Qur'an and are corrected by it, they shade the truth and so have to be discarded.

Allah is compassionate and merciful. That is a wondrous revelation, for certainly so sovereign a Lord does not have to go kindly with creatures. Yet such kindness is the nature of the Lord of the worlds. His compassion and mercy are not cloaks that he dons on occasion, and so may easily cast aside. They express his inmost being, which is goodness without limit or division. To say that he is king of judgment day is to remind all who hear the Qur'an that right and wrong will separate. The current commingling of the two is only temporary. When history ends, the great Lord will deal with the good and the wicked decisively. Dispensing reward and punishment with complete justice, he will vindicate all who have clung to his word, followed the Prophet, and chosen the path of righteous deeds.

The proper response to Allah, on learning of his being and message, is praise. When one experiences the lordship of the creator, one can only exclaim in wonder and thanksgiving. He stretched the heavens and cast forth the stars. He hung the sun and the moon, and he sends the tides. From a clot of blood he fashioned human beings, his images and vice-gerents. He is the Lord, the overseer, the ruler, and the judge of all creation. Praise him, for his wondrous majesty!

The mood here is familiar to Christians and Jews from the Psalms. When the human spirit is bowled over by the perception of the divine majesty, it can only break forth in praise. Arabs of Muhammad's day, like human beings in most times and places throughout history, lived close enough to nature to be bowled over easily. In the clarity of the desert air, day and night, they could experience the vastness of the divine mystery. The blazing sun, the endless sand, the pellucid nights filled with stars—all tended to hush the spirit and precipitate awe.

The one responsible for the grandeur of the natural world is the only one worthy of worship. Worship is complete dedication. The more we understand this central human action and need, the more we appreciate monotheism. We can only give our complete response to the divinity responsible for the whole of creation, and this divinity must be one, because otherwise it would be less whole than what it has made. In the light of biblical and Qur'anic revelation, worship is the model for all human devotion. Monogamy is a faint reflection of proper worship, like it in being single-minded, undivided at heart. Islam did not develop the biblical notion that the people called by God are like God's spouse. Allah is far too exalted for that. Between him and human beings lie only the bridges that he laid down: the Qur'an, prophets such as Abraham, Moses, Jesus, and Muhammad, and angels carrying messages. Allah could not have a divine Son. Nothing could partake of his divinity. He is not a divinity intent on sharing his substance or fashioning a partner for covenantal love. So the "alone" of this call to worship reflects a solitude in God. Self-sufficient, splendid and complete in all ways, Allah was sublimely merciful even to create human beings.

Still, human beings can pray to Allah for help. Their response to him is not only selfless worship but also needy petition. Allah knows the abjectness of humankind and hears its requests. Men and women have to turn to Allah for their deepest needs, because there is no other recourse. At times Islam has been fatalistic about this reality. "If Allah wills it" has preceded or followed even banal expressions of hope. What Allah wills is sure to occur, and what Allah rejects is sure to remain rejected.

For what ought human beings to pray? For all their needs, but especially for fidelity. If Allah guides us to the straight path, everything else in our lives will turn out well. But we depend on Allah for this guidance. It is nothing certain, on which we may presume. The straight path, elaborated in the Qur'an, marks people as favored. If they can do what is right, they carry the blessing of God. Conversely, those who have incurred the wrath of Allah wander off the straight path, onto the byways of destruction. Going astray, they risk ending up in the fire. So the most basic prayer is for guidance, direction, what we might call wisdom. Those whom Allah favors (those whose prayers he incites and answers) can discern the straight path and muster the courage to follow it. Those who live circuitously, following their own will or alien gods, are foolish, weak, sick unto death.

Christian readers of the Qur'an do best when they suspend critical judgment and let the power of the passionate imagery for God sweep over them. Here is a scripture as convinced as their own that God is truly God: supreme, sovereign, fully in control. Equally, here is a scripture proclaiming the goodness of God—the divine mercy and compassion. For the Qur'an, Allah is as near as the pulse at one's throat (the carotid). Transcending the farthest galaxies, he yet moves in the circulation of the lymph. So, like the biblical God, in all ways he holds the primacy and priority. In all ways true religion is seconding his initiatives. And accepting this, living by this, does not suppress the creature but fulfills it. The nearer one comes to God, the more fully one enters upon one's own selfhood and freedom. Muslims could easily make their own the Christian liturgical prayer, "God, to serve whom is to reign," help us in this our affliction. This, our affliction, might be a present trial, or it might be the simple state of creaturehood, which for us humans is bound to be painful. It might be the burden of mortality, or the burden of loving God but not being able to embrace him decisively, with every nerve and sinew. From the Qur'an, millions of Muslims have drawn counsel much like that on the lips of many Christian saints: there is no exaggerating the goodness of God. In the case of true divinity, there is no hyperbole.

Sufi Love

Though Islam does not develop the notion that the faithful are the bride of Allah, it does make human love an analogy for the intercourse between Allah and the pious, mystical soul. This analogy was important to many Sufi poets, among whom the thirteenth century master Rumi stands out. The Sufis probably arose as a protest movement, collecting people who wanted a more intense spiritual life than what was flourishing after Islam had conquered much of the Middle East and become a theocracy. Just as Christian monasticism spread rapidly after the Constantinian era, when the church became a political power, so Sufism spread as a somewhat countercultural effort to affirm otherworldly rather than this-worldly values. The Sufis were not monks, though they did form "brotherhoods," led by masters able to give instruction in prayer. Islam, like Judaism, always frowned on celibacy, and Muhammad was remembered as having enjoined "no monkery." Rumi founded the influential Mevlevi Brotherhood or Order, and his splendid poetry adorns the Persian effloresence of Islamic culture, one of its finest.

One of Rumi's most famous figures pictures the person passionate for God as a forlorn reed: "Hearken to this Reed forlorn, breathing, ever since 'twas torn from its rushy bed, a strain of impassioned love and pain. The secret of my song, though near, none can see and none can hear. Oh, for a friend to know the sign and mingle all his soul with mine! 'Tis the flame of Love that fired me, 'tis the wine of Love inspired me. Wouldst thou learn how lovers bleed, hearken, hearken to the Reed!"[6]

The Sufis got into trouble with the guardians of Muslim orthodoxy whenever they seemed to establish any parity between the human spirit and God, or whenever they did not beat the drum that the divine is wholly transcendent. In the worst case, the mystic Al-Hallaj proclaimed himself one with Allah and so was executed. Rumi is ambiguous enough to fend off accusations of impropriety. The forlorn reed is humanity itself, as well as the especially ardent soul, which has come from God and senses that its present state is a loss of an aboriginal unity. Pascal spoke of the human person as a thinking reed, perhaps building on the promise of Second Isaiah, applied to Jesus from earliest Christian times, that "the bruised reed he will not break." Here the point seems not so much the frailty of the vessel carrying human thought as the likeness of a reed torn from the river bed to a human being apart from God. God is the ground, the matrix, of human existence, without which there is no stability or sure meaning. However they describe their situation, whether or not they invoke imagery of a fall or original sin, sensitive men and women the world over speak of a loss, an alienation, a profound instinct that what ought to be whole (because it was whole "in the beginning") has been ruptured.

Rumi's reed expresses love and pain in its every breath. As the basis for music (wind instruments), the reed is played by its love and pain, sending forth a heart-rending song. So the love seems to be primarily longing and desire. It is not the benevolent care of a parent, or even the intellectual satisfaction of a friend, that Rumi calls to mind. It is the lover separated from the beloved, the lover feeling that half of the self is missing.

Peculiar to this case of religious love, though, is the deity that none can see or hear. The explanation for the pangs scoring the heart in this case is near enough but imperceptible. This is the realization, common in most descriptions of the spirit's ascent of Mount Carmel, that nothing in human experience can serve up God, capture God, render God adequately. The very simplicity of God defeats human complexity, so the human spirit intuits that it must die for its love. Only when it gains a different state, a different being, may it hope to be up to its project, its constitutive longing. The friend who could appreciate this state of affairs would be a true friend indeed—a bondsman for the journey. Sharing passion for God, he or she would fortify Rumi's soul. Another possibility is that Rumi longs for divinity itself to note the signs of his love, take mercy, and effect the commingling he desires—the mystical union. This would be a bold possibility, because no one came closer to God than Muhammad, and the most that Muhammad became was God's *rasul:* announcer, proclaimer.

The third stanza focuses on the love itself, perhaps meaning to make love, this so potent energy, a very presence of God. If this poem were Christian, one could speculate about the Holy Spirit, pouring forth into believers' hearts the love that is divine life. Since it is not, the most one can suspect is that Rumi thought of love as one of the many valid names of Allah—perhaps the most important bead on the rosary. Love is a flame, turning all the soul aglow, but also branding it. Love is a wine, taking the poet out of himself, intoxicating him. As he experiences it, this reed singing so passionately, so mournfully, teaches how much suffering love of God entails. The bleeding of human lovers, their

sense of being raked by love, is a pale figure for what the soul in love
with God goes through. To be apart is sore hurt. Each thought of the
beloved, each wish to behold, embrace, or share, opens the sore anew.
And because the beloved in this case is God, the pain is constant, fixed
in the ground or quintessence of the soul.

When it comes to Christian mystical theology, data such as this
poem of Rumi's are heartening. What Christians experience in their
searches for God occurs the world over. The romantic hue is strongest
in mystical literatures that assume a personal deity who calls human
beings to intersubjective communication. Love requires dialogue, contact with mind and heart. And love naturally thinks of touches, embraces, an intercourse that would be both simple and comprehensive.
That is why the Song of Songs, which apparently arose as secular love
poetry, finally seemed to fit the biblical canon. For Christians who
believe that God is the sole source of any human being's fulfillment, the
Song, and the many other testimonies from people passionate about
God the world over, is immensely helpful. Instinctively, those who have
known intense human love realize that love of God must be similar.
Because the human desire and delight have been the most significant
experiences in the lover's life, they have to point to what fully successful religion would be.

During some periods of Christian history passion got a bad name in
theological circles, especially among moral theologians influenced by
Greek notions of *apatheia:* self-possession, freedom from desire. And
much eastern ethics, wrestling with the connections between desire
and karmic bondage, has also frowned on passion. But Rumi, other
Muslim mystics, and a great chorus of Christian saints have thought
otherwise. To their mind, the crux was the experience of God they
either sought or had received. Actually, what most of them realized was
that even their ardent seeking was a significant finding. To long for God
was already to feel God, in the paradoxical mode of the divine absence.

Here the philosophical theologians helped, because they hastened
to say that God can never be absent, since without God's grants of
existence any creature would tumble back into nothingness. But the
mystics wanted more: help with the emotional losses they were suffering, support in their search for a God who would take them to heart,
give them the kiss that would satisfy their souls. Rumi's metaphor of the
reed mixes both the natural and the personal aspects of the mystical
longing for God. As torn from its rushy bed, the reed is like a bit of

flotsam threatening to drift away. As singing its plaint, the reed is like the human being giving voice to all that fills and afflicts it. Together, the two aspects convey the totality of the mystic's longing. Everything that lovers of God are or imagine focuses in their poetry, their prayer, often making these an offering of simple heartache.

Almsgiving and Pilgrimage

The five principal duties or "pillars" of Islam are to confess Muslim faith (epitomized in the verse, "There is no God but God, and Muhammad is God's Prophet"), pray five times a day (facing Mecca), fast during the (lunar) month of Ramadan, give alms, and make the pilgrimage to Mecca. All of these duties are social, in the sense that all tie Muslims into the community of the faithful ("the House of Islam"), but the last two bear most directly on solidarity and justice.

Almsgiving is not optional in Islam. Against the background of clan society, helping those in need was essential to survival (there were no welfare agencies). Muhammad tried to broaden the social instinct of his fellow Arabs, substituting their new faith for old tribal loyalties. All Muslims (submitters to Allah) were sisters and brothers. So any Muslim had a claim on the help of all others. Naturally, as Islam grew to include hundreds of millions of believers this sense of solidarity became problematic. But the common practice of expecting productive members of the community to contribute from their income to the support of the less fortunate helped to maintain a sense of brotherhood and sisterhood.

For Muhammad himself, widows and orphans were special objects of pity, and so special foci of community care. The amount of the alms (which became a sort of tax) varied somewhat, but the usual fraction was two or three percent of one's income. Representatives of the local community collected the alms (which people normally gave voluntarily, without compulsion) and saw that it reached those most in need. The average Muslim believed that God expected almsgiving and always knew who complied and who did not.

The closest that Christians have come to this sense of ratifying social solidarity through almsgiving is the tithe that some churches have required. Otherwise, Christian communities have depended on the notion that charity is so important a virtue that all good believers would give generously. The tithe, amounting to ten percent of one's income, is a generous but defensible fraction. The major problem has occurred when the institutional side of the church has taken the major share of Christian almsgiving for its own operational needs and the poor have received only a small fraction.

The pilgrimage to Mecca has been a more dramatic way for Muslims to fortify their sense of worldwide solidarity, though in recent years antagonisms between Iranians and Saudis have marred the annual celebrations, as have numerous deaths due to terrorist attacks or stampedes. Traditionally, the time of pilgrimage was a time for any Muslims in conflict to set aside their differences. Mecca, the birthplace of Islam, has been the holiest soil and so a sanctuary. Pilgrims have dressed in similar garb, minimizing distinctions between Africans and Malaysians, women and men. They have gone through the same traditional devotional practices, recalling the deeds of Abraham, venerating the black stone at the Ka'ba, the central shrine, and in many other ways trying to create what the anthropologist Victor Turner called communitas: the rare experience of easy acceptance and bonding, due to the strength of people's most idealistic values, which the special ("liminal") time of pilgrimage has allowed to pour forth.

An anticipation of the pilgrimage to Mecca (hajj), created by the Egyptian novelist Najib Mahfuz, conveys some of these idealistic values: "It was a joyful day of leave-taking. Ridwan had hoped that God would choose him to make the holy Pilgrimage to Mecca and Medina and this year so He had. Every one knew that this was the day when he would leave for the Holy Land. His house was filled with well-wishers, lifelong friends and devout Muslims. They clustered in his modest room which had so often echoed with their pious and friendly discussions. They chatted about the Pilgrimage and their reminiscences of it, their voices rising from every corner of the room and mixing with a trail of smoke billowing up from the brazier. They told tales of the modern Pilgrimage and those of bye-gone days and rehearsed holy traditions and beautiful verses concerning it. One man with a melodious voice chanted verses from the Holy Qur'an and then they listened to a long and eloquent speech by Ridwan that expressed his heart's goodness. A pious friend wished him a happy and safe return, to which Husseini beamed and replied in his most gentle manner: 'Please, my friend, don't remind me of my return. Anyone who visits God's house with a longing for home deserves to have God deny him his reward, ignore his prayers and destroy his happiness."[7]

To go to God's house is to go to the center of the world. In each mosque there is a niche pointing the way to Mecca. Not only do Muslims pray in the direction of Mecca; if they are pious, like Ridwan, their thoughts are always moving toward it. In many places the chance to make the pilgrimage comes by lot. The ordinary person is too poor to pay for the journey, so the community sponsors a few pilgrims to represent it, and the choice is by lot. The usual understanding of the obligation to make the pilgrimage is that one has to do it at least once in one's lifetime, unless circumstances (physical disability, poverty) make that impossible. The pilgrimage is both a duty and a privilege. Muslims have the duty to come to God's house as an act of homage—a holy courtesy. But they have the more significant privilege of visiting the center of Islam, where the Prophet first received the revelations of the Qur'an and fashioned the House of Islam. The personal benefit of moving through such hallowed precincts far outweighs any costs or difficulties one may incur. The experience of being part of a vast throng passionate for God overwhelms most pilgrims, at least on their first visit, and converts such as Malcolm X have reported having their hearts cleansed by finding that all prejudice and bitterness washed away.

The Christian analogue for pilgrimage to Mecca is uncertain. Most Christians would consider a trip to the Holy Land (meaning Israel) attractive, inasmuch as it would acquaint them with the hills that Jesus saw and the streets that he walked, but they would not consider it obligatory. Some Roman Catholics have made trips to Rome a pilgrimage, and in medieval Europe numerous shrines to saints drew heavy traffic. Chaucer has described the pilgrimage to Canterbury in less flattering terms than what we saw in the mind of the Egyptian pilgrim setting out for Mecca, but that does not mean that many pious Christians did not strengthen their faith. Even today pilgrims to Marian shrines in Europe and Latin America often report strong religious experiences.

Still, Christianity has not been tied to a particular place the way that Jews have been tied to Jerusalem and Muslims to Mecca. The center of Christian faith has been a risen Lord freed of all geographical boundaries. When Gentiles entered the Christian church, and its center shifted from Jerusalem (destroyed in 70 A.D.) to Rome (the center of the empire), Christians left behind any obligation to focus their faith on a particular city. There was no land that could not become holy, and even though Christian imagination invested Israel with a special sanctity, that remained a matter of piety rather than a requirement of doctrinal or practical faith. There was no requirement to visit any pilgrimage site. The requirement was to visit the risen Lord regularly, at the assembly in one's given locale.

So Christians interested in dialogue with pious Muslims might indulge or develop a bit of holy envy. Muslims are fortunate to have a given place, a given ritual, that reminds them forcefully each year of their common roots. On the other hand, Muslims might develop a bit of holy envy for the concreteness of the stories about Jesus in the Christian Bible, which made his native milieu so easy to imagine that much Christian prayer pictured him standing by the Sea of Galilee or entering Jerusalem seated on a donkey. When these images dominated the common liturgy, Christians shared a brief pilgrimage of their own, leaving their workaday imaginations to visit the places where God had accomplished their salvation.

Women

All of the world religions have been problematic for women. No major tradition can pass muster if the call is to meet today's egalitarian standards. Everywhere—China, Israel, Christian Europe, India, Japan, Arabia—patriarchal cultures have shaped religious messages, ensuring that women would be the subordinate sex. Sometimes subordination has gone hand in hand with a peculiar elevation: femininity stereotyped as more naturally religious (passive, peaceful). Other times subordination has been complete: a version of humanity more seductive, even dirty, than what one finds in masculinity. It is hard to find a winner, when the contest is for a religion that has treated women fully kindly. Even when, on their own terms, given religious traditions loved women and tried to protect them, those terms continued to be patriarchal and so condescending if not ignorant.

Islam is neither the worst nor the best of the world religions when it comes to women. Nowadays fundamentalist Islam draws the special ire of feminists, but if one considers history as a whole, Muhammad emerges as a champion of women, against the abusive practices of his time, and the Muslim ideal for family life grants women considerable dignity. Still, because the Qur'an itself offers a patriarchal view of women, men's rule over women seems to be encoded in Islamic revelation.

Consider the following verses from the surah (4) traditionally entitled "Women": "Men have authority over women because Allah has made the one superior to the other, and because they spend their wealth to maintain them. Good women are obedient. They guard their unseen parts because Allah has guarded them. As for those from whom you fear disobedience, admonish them and send them to beds apart and beat them. Then if they obey you, take no further action against them. Allah is high, supreme."[8]

The opening verse, giving the bottom line, could not be more plain: the subordination of women is part of God's plan. Male authority is not simply an accident of history, or a product of the greater physical strength that men usually enjoy. It rests in a superiority intended by God. Whether "superiority" here implies greater moral worth is not certain. It might mean simply "having the role of the social superior," because Islam has always taught that men and women have equal opportunity to gain the Garden and need equally to fear the Fire. Traditions to the effect that more men gain the Garden than women, and that women preponderate in the Fire because of their disobedience to their husbands, do not have Qur'anic status. Still, those accrediting such traditions could believe that they were simply filling out the implications of verses such as these that we are now examining.

Men spend money on women, and because of that, Arab culture judged that men had the right to control women. Traditional Arab culture, like most other traditional (patriarchal) cultures, did not allow women equal economic opportunity. True, the widow Khadija, Muhammad's first wife, owned a caravan company and was much wealthier than he. But she was the exception to the general rule, and as the Prophet (who started out as her employee) grew in stature, he came to dominate their relationship. So women had no choice in the matter of having men spend money on them. It was the only way that they could survive. When they were girls, females depended on their fathers. In maturity, they depended on their husbands. And in older age, they depended on their sons (if they had not begotten sons they were in peril). The entire cast of society made women dependents. But the equation of financial dependence with submission to men in all other areas could be pernicious, making women little better than slaves. Yes, affection, and women's wit, usually worked against the worst abuses. The Qur'an, and subsequent Muslim legal codes, provided for women's rights in inheritance (less than men's) and divorce (skimpy—men could divorce women at will). But none of this made women remotely the equals of men. Indeed, even in the matter of the custody of children in the event of divorce women's rights were less than men's.

The notion that good women are obedient summarized the Muslim ideal. Other authorities might go on to say that good women are intelligent, beautiful, loving, pious, and other desirable things, but the crux was women's obedience to the men who dominated their lives. As Allah stood to men, so did men stand to women. Thus women's submission to men was meritorious religiously. In one notable image, women were dragged into the Garden by the umbilical cords of their children, and they fell into the Fire because they were not docile to their husbands. The sign of the end of time was the rule of women over men— the complete overturning of the natural order.

The tradition of veiling women, and even of keeping them in purdah, has depended on verses like the one about the need for women to guard their unseen parts. Most Muslim cultures have considered women a temptation to men (as many other cultures have), so having women wear modest clothing has been considered essential, lest women occasion men's sin. Today the veil is a lodestone for debate about women's rights in Islam. Many countries, moved by fundamentalist tides, have reinstituted veiling for women, and regularly it serves as a prime criterion for a woman's religiosity (in the eyes of fundamentalists).[9]

The punishments for women's even causing men to fear that they would be disobedient are startling: banishment from the marital bed, and beating (if need be). The Qur'an allows men up to four wives, if they can provide for that many (in affection, as well as finances), so the banishment wore more on women than on men. Monogamy soon became the Muslim ideal, but the Prophet himself had supported numerous wives (some apparently through marriages designed more to liberate them from oppressive circumstance than to put them in his own service), and debates about modernizing legal codes have generated acrimonious reactions to the proposal that monogamy be made mandatory. Apparent scriptural permission to beat recalcitrant wives has worked in Islam all the horrors that it has worked in Christianity—

horrors that only present-day feminist sensibilities have dragged from the underside of world history and shown to be deeply abusive.

Christians have little to brag about when it comes to the treatment of women, and so a sensitive dialogue between Christians and Muslims ought to bring forth mutual support in confessing past sins and repenting. Certainly there are also many things to celebrate in the history of both traditions—above all, many holy women who have witnessed to the surpassing goodness of God. In both traditions women have regularly provided the heart of the community's faith, sacrificing themselves that men might study and raising children to stand tall under heaven. The limitations on women's participation in formal religion, which continue in both traditions today, sour the tastebuds of egalitarians, but once again historians have to note that underlings have often outwitted their oppressors. In Islam a special burden has been women's separation from higher education, even in the area of religion. That changed in the twentieth century in many of the countries that were modernizing, but the new fundamentalists have sometimes called such change into doubt. The early marriage of women in traditional Muslim societies, and the heavy childbearing, further depressed most women's possibilities, making the fate of being born female much less happy than being born male.

Christians taking their own sins of sexism to heart find that they too have miles to go before they can sleep with good consciences. Few churches allow women full access to authority and ministry, and many churches have yet to work out either non-sexist liturgies or non-sexist versions of scripture. Thus Christians can consider the Qur'anic surah on women a sharp reminder of what women everywhere have suffered at the hands of religion. That could make calls for radical change in churches such as the Roman Catholic easier to hear and take to heart.

War

If relations between the sexes are a major issue of social justice, so are attitudes toward peace and war. The Qur'an sends a mixed message about warfare. On the one hand, it urges Muslims to unite against the infidel, when the latter would oppose the spread of Islam. Muhammad believed that his community had a commission from God to spread its faith. Those who accepted this commission, allowing Muslims to take over their realms and offer their people faith, would be treated well. Those who opposed this commission, claiming that they wanted to go their own ways in peace, would suffer hard times. The choice lay with the potential enemy. If outsiders gave Muslims no quarrel, they could expect subordinate yet dignified status in a new Muslim regime. Because spreading the faith was a divine mandate, however, resort to arms and warfare could be a holy necessity. *Jihad* (struggle) has meant both interior warfare against one's own vices and exterior warfare against the enemies of Islam. In the latter meaning, it has amounted to "holy war": war supposedly sanctioned by God; war in which death for serving the Muslim cause sent one directly to the Garden.

The other part of the Qur'anic message about war and peace has been to support peacemaking wherever possible. Thus we find in surah 49: "If two parties of believers take up arms the one against the other, make peace between them. If either of them commits aggression against the other, fight against the aggressors till they submit to Allah's judgement. When they submit make peace between them in equity and justice. Allah loves those who act in justice."[10]

We note first that here the conflict concerns believers. In struggles among fellow Muslims, the entire effort should be to accomplish peace and justice. The aggressor comes under a cloud, and the rest of the community, or the proper authorities, should bend all efforts to punish the aggressor until peace returns. In fact Muslim nations have been unable to achieve this ideal, because they have created no governing authority overseeing the entire House of Islam. Yet the unseemliness of believers warring with believers has continued to exert a useful pressure. Even in recent warfare such as that between Iran and Iraq, many Muslims have felt that something shameful was occurring.

The great blight in the Muslim community has been the division between Sunnis and Shiites. Sunnis are the great majority, but Shiites are numerous enough to make their voices and guns heard. This division goes back to the time just after the Prophet's death, when disputes arose about the line of succession to power. Those now known as Shiites felt that inheritance should follow the Prophet's blood line. Those now known as Sunnis did not agree, following the general Arab custom of selecting the person thought best equipped (or possessing the greatest political clout). When this dispute turned bloody, with charges of assassination ringing on both sides, the House of Islam settled in for centuries of bitterness. Much of the volatility of Iranian Islam becomes understandable when one appreciates this background. As the center of Shiite traditions, Iran has felt it had to wage an uphill struggle against the rest of the Muslim world.

The parallel for Christians is easy to find. The wars between Catholics and Protestants, and the enmities between eastern Christians and western, fall into the same shameful category as the strife in Islam. Christians have slain other Christians, seldom for completely religious reasons, but often under the pretext that the enemy was dirty with heresy. Real hatred has flowed back and forth, as continues to be the case today in Northern Ireland. Fortunately, the ecumenical movement of the twentieth century has given all Christians desiring a better, more defensible spirituality reasons for hope. Nowadays, the hatreds between Protestants and Catholics in hell-holes such as Northern Ireland are repudiated throughout the body of Christ.

When it comes to Christian parallels to Muslim *jihad* the obvious instance is the crusades. As Jews who were slain almost accidentally, for sport, when crusaders marched through Jewish quarters en route to confront "the Turk" realized to their horror, the bloodlust that drove many crusaders had little to do with defensible religion. Recovering the Holy Land was often merely an excuse to lash out at everything that seemed to threaten Christian culture and hegemony. "Our" cause became so righteous that we could slay "them" as though they were fiends loosed from hell.

We have already noted the deep problems that the doctrine of election or special covenant can create, and here we need only reinforce what we said earlier. Few religious wars have been pleasing to God. God, as the Qur'an here makes clear, loves those who act in justice. Real justice seldom requires bloodshed. To use power to try to secure justice is to run great risks, and when one's use of power involves bloodshed, the great likelihood is that those risks include the wrath of God.

"The wrath of God" is not God's own lashing out in power, God's own resort to bloodshed. Under this traditional figure, writers from biblical times on have tried to express their intuition that some things anger God, sicken God, are so repugnant that God has to wonder about the decision to create the people involved. How God expresses this reaction, what it means in terms of world history, is beyond our reckoning. The best Christian theology has interpreted the line " 'Vengeance is mine,' saith the Lord," to mean that all will become right on judgment day. The worst Christian theology has thought that God's representatives ought to take vengeance on infidels or wrongdoers in God's name. Nowadays the ecumenical majority of Christians think that sending people to the stake for religious deviance contradicts the gospel of Christ.

It is not clear that the majority of Muslims feels this way about dealing with Muslim deviants, as the worldwide reaction to the Ayatollah Khomeini's death-threat against the novelist Salman Rushdie indicates. While some Muslims have been appalled at this threat, thinking it barbaric and unreligious, others have backed it enthusiastically. When people think that they have cornered the market on God's truth, and that they must defend God's honor, their logic can be frightfully clear: wipe out those who besmirch the divine goodness, who are offensive in the sight of the divine holiness. Even when one can dismiss many of the psychodynamics at work in such cases as forces of repression and inferiority, the religious question remains. How can any sane religion cause people to think that they can act as executioners sent by God?

The significance of all this for a Catholic spirituality striving to mature to the demands of today's global culture is not hard to imagine. All of the traditional reasons for spotlighting the Jesus who was meek and humble of heart now come to the fore reinforced. Violence should be the last resort of people wanting to live as Christ lived and forward Christ's cause. The first and constant instinct should be that God will take care of any affronts to God's honor, and so that we human beings ought to limit our sanctions to what is necessary for good order.

Within the community of Christ itself, where forgiveness ought to be prominent, good order requires only that people make loving their neighbors as themselves their political practice. Again and again, communities that accept this discipline find that they can tolerate considerable diversity about both belief and practice. That does not mean that there can be no heresy or grounds for excommunication. It does mean that accusations of heresy and moves to excommunication should be so rare as to interest mainly scholars nosing into curios.

Many will say that this is a woefully optimistic reading of current Christian history, but in our eyes it is based on the church's own woeful past. When has schism ever benefited the cause of Christ? Who looks upon the sunderings of the eleventh century, when east and west fell apart, or of the sixteenth century, when "Papists" and "Protestants" became epithets carrying venom, as times of which to be proud? All of the prophetic religions, Judaism as well as Christianity and Islam, have so often botched the mission of announcing God's call for repentance that all ought to stay far away from the temptation to judge and punish in God's name. All have fought, hurt others, and split their communities so regularly that they have made it difficult to believe in their God. So all should stand abashed by the scandal they have given, and all should be receptive to a future spirituality that makes judgment nearly completely a mysterious affair hidden in God.

NOTES

1. *Seder Eliyahu Rabbah,* 23; in HAMMER ON THE ROCK: A MIDRASH READER, ed. Nahum N. Glatzer (New York: Schocken, 1962), p. 89.

2. Wendy M. Wright, SACRED DWELLING (New York: Crossroad, 1990), p. 45.

3. *Pirke Aboth,* 3:11–12; in THE ETHICS OF THE TALMUD: SAYINGS OF THE FATHERS, ed. R. Travers Herford (New York: Schocken, 1962), pp. 76–77.

4. *Taan.,* 22a; in EVERYMAN'S TALMUD, ed. A. Cohen (New York: Schocken, 1975), p. 204.

5. *The Koran,* trans. N. J. Dawood (Baltimore: Penguin, 1968), p. 15.

6. A. J. Arberry, SUFISM (New York: Harper & Row, 1970), p. 111.

7. Kenneth Cragg and Marston Speight, ISLAM FROM WITHIN (Belmont: Wadsworth, 1980), p. 58.

8. *The Koran,* trans. Dawood, pp. 360–361.

9. For general background on Muslim cultures, see Isma'il R. al Faruqi and Lois Lamya'al Faruqi, THE CULTURAL ATLAS OF ISLAM (New York: Macmillan, 1986). On women's spirituality in Islam, see Saadia Khawar Khan Chishti, "Female Spirituality in Islam," in ISLAMIC SPIRITUALITY: FOUNDATIONS, ed. Seyyed Hossein Nasr (New York: Crossroad, 1987), pp. 199–218. For recent attitudes in India, see Martha Stevenson, "Hers: Ladies' Compartment," *The New York Times Magazine,* July 1, 1990, pp. 10, 32.

10. *The Koran,* trans. Dawood, p. 268.

Chapter 6

Methodological Issues

Faith

In the first chapter we dealt briefly with methodological issues when we introduced the notions of "the history of religions" and "Catholic spirituality." In this chapter we reflect more leisurely on the relations between these two partners to the dialogue that we have been sponsoring. If one of the church fathers were writing this chapter, the subtitle might be: "Despoiling the Egyptians."

When thinking of how Christians ought to use pagan wisdom, many church fathers called to mind the account of the exodus. After God had delivered the Hebrews and caused the Egyptians who had pursued them to perish, the Hebrews helped themselves to the arms and other treasures that the Egyptians had left. This imagery seems too self-centered, triumphalist, and harsh to be appropriate today, when Christians ought to be sensitive to all the workings of God's grace outside of institutional Christianity. Still, something in it comes close to our intent, when we urge those interested in Catholic spirituality to attend to the findings of historians of religion.

That something is the instinct to adapt what others have developed to one's own purposes. In this case, the others are generally professors in secular universities, and what they have developed are fascinating descriptions of how human beings have behaved and thought, when they created their various religious complexes. As noted in our Introduction, such professors usually prescind from the question of personal faith (what this ought to mean for the person studying their data). In contrast, Catholic spirituality, at least in our understanding, depends completely on faith. Unless Jesus is its great treasure, no spirituality to our liking can be called Christian. So it might seem obvious that the

140

ultimate disposition of materials from the history of religions would involve their correlation with and submission to Christian criteria, when Christians are trying to take them to heart, but in reality several factors conspire to make this far from obvious. One prominent factor, curiously enough, is the lack of personal faith in God apparently obtaining among people in divinity schools who work at the history of religions—indeed, who work at religious studies generally, or even theology.

Such an assessment of the personal dispositions of many divinity school personnel comes from no less prominent and interesting a figure than Wendy Doniger O'Flaherty, Mircea Eliade Professor of the History of Religions at the University of Chicago Divinity School. In an interview focused on her recent book *Other People's Myths,* Professor O'Flaherty first opines that most of the people working in religious studies are personally interested in religion: "I think the people who study religion are usually interested in religion. You selected religion instead of physics or English because you're curious about the things that the people who write books in the field of religion are curious about. And at some level that has to be personal. I don't mean that we're all seekers after truth; I mean that we like to spend our hours talking about moral questions, theological questions, questions of old-fashioned philosophy. Not the things they do nowadays in philosophy, which is mostly linguistic analysis."

Then, after the interviewer has tried to summarize this drift by interjecting "What is reality?" O'Flaherty moves along to make a remarkable statement: "Yes—what is reality—all those heavies, those real serious heavies. Whether people believe in God or belong to an organized religion is, I think, totally irrelevant. I think most of the people I've worked with, both in the faculty and students, probably do neither of those. That doesn't stop you from being the sort of person who is interested in human questions of an old-fashioned kind, questions that never get answered—the meaning of life and death, and what have you."[1]

Now, several reactions come to mind. First, it is somewhat anomalous that many of the leading historians of religion teach in divinity schools—mainly an accident of the history of universities such as Chicago and Harvard, which decided to lump all formal dealings with religion in the divinity schools that they had inherited from their religious origins. Second, it is important to realize that O'Flaherty is simply reporting one person's impressions, and that both belief in God and belonging to an organized religion are slippery matters, not always perceptible on the basis of people's external behavior, or even of their academic discussions. Third, O'Flaherty is not trying to separate scholarship in the history of religions from an interest in existential matters traditionally handled by religion—far from it. She stands against the frequent trivialization of big questions by analytical philosophy, stands for the permanent validity of those big questions.

But, fourth, there is a willingness to locate people's responses to big questions on the level of talking about them. This is typical of academicians, who are always talking, and who tend to leave aside the personal decisions that elude talk (that are deep enough to require silence and personal confrontation with ultimate reality). In other words, though few historians of religion would agree (when it came to scholarly analysis) that religion is a private affair, most take a hands-off approach to the faith or non-faith of their students and colleagues. This approach is understandable and intelligent, inasmuch as it simplifies the academic study of religion and the politics of colleagueship. On the other hand, it tends to make faith appear to be something optional, when in fact it cannot be.

In Bernard Lonergan's analysis of religion, the real questions go far below the level of talk. The level of talk concerns itself with data (experience) and hypotheses (insights about how the data might cohere). To get to the level of judgment (what is so about the data, in contrast to what might be so), one has to enter the thickets of reflective understanding, the depths of which include convictions about one's own capacity to know objective reality. Even more ultimate, however, is the question that comes after well-wrought judgments: What am I going to do about this judgment (of truth or falsity) to which I have committed myself? If Lonergan's analysis of human consciousness is valid, this question for decision and action is a moral imperative—something that one cannot lay aside, simply because academic talk is not interested in it (or is afraid of it).[2]

Christian spirituality is concerned with data and hypotheses from the history of religions, but ultimately it is more concerned with judgments and decisions. For Christian spirituality (any spirituality) is a matter of following a path through life—a path laid out by faith. One cannot take an object of faith such as Jesus seriously and not deal with all the rearrangements of data, hypotheses, judgments, and even emotions that commitment to Jesus implies. It would be more than anomalous to practice Christian spirituality without faith; it would be contradictory. So, history of religions on the model that Professor O'Flaherty represents as typical and seems to approve is something that those working on Christian spirituality have to adapt to their own enterprise, and such an adaptation will be radical in the measure that such workers experience what the saints of their traditions have experienced: the complete relativization of all secular knowledge that occurs when one experiences the divine mystery intensely.

Consider, for example, the following declaration by John of the Cross: "The drink of highest wisdom makes her [the human soul] forget all worldly things. And it seems that her previous knowledge, and even all the knowledge of the world, in comparison with this knowledge is pure ignorance. For a better understanding of this, it should be known that the most formal cause of the soul's knowing nothing of the world when in this state [of mystical contact by God] is that she is being informed with supernatural knowledge, in the presence of which all natural and political knowledge of the world is ignorance rather than knowledge. When the soul is brought into this lofty knowing, she understands by means of it that all other knowledge which has not the taste of this knowledge is not knowledge but ignorance, and that there is nothing to know in it. She declares the truth of the Apostle's words, that what is greater wisdom in the sight of men is foolishness before God [1 Cor. 3:19]. Hence she asserts that she no longer knew anything after drinking of that divine wisdom. And this truth (that the wisdom of men and of the whole world is pure ignorance and unworthy of being known) cannot be understood except by this favor of God's presence in the soul, by which He communicates His wisdom and comforts her with the drink of love that she may behold this truth clearly . . . the reason is that in the excess of the lofty wisdom of God the lowly wisdom of men is ignorance. The natural sciences themselves and the very works of God, when set beside what it is to know God, are like ignorance. For where God is unknown nothing is known."[3]

The Sacred

Wendy Doniger O'Flaherty was trained in Sanskrit to study classical Indian culture. Under the influence of Mircea Eliade, with whom she taught at the University of Chicago Divinity School, she became interested in the history of religions: the wider swath of humanity's search for ultimate meaning, within which one can place Hinduism and the rest of classical Indian culture. For Eliade, the overriding interest was manifestations of the sacred. Thus, at the beginning of his three-volume work on the history of religious ideas, Eliade wrote: "For the historian of religions, *every* manifestation of the sacred is important: every rite, every myth, every belief or divine figure reflects the experience of the sacred and hence implies the notions of *being,* of *meaning,* and of *truth.* As I observed on another occasion, 'it is difficult to imagine how the human mind could function without the conviction that there is something irreducibly *real* in the world; and it is impossible to imagine how consciousness could appear without conferring a *meaning* on man's impulses and experiences. Consciousness of a real and meaningful world is intimately connected with the discovery of the sacred. Through experience of the sacred, the human mind has perceived the difference between what reveals itself as being real, powerful, rich, and meaningful and what lacks these qualities, that is, the chaotic and dangerous flux of things, their fortuitous and senseless appearances and disappearances.' "[4]

Many peoples have described their experiences of the sacred in terms of divine action. It has been the Great Spirit, or Allah, or Heaven, or the local god of the river who wrought their perception of something extraordinary. For Christians, the whole matter of how to evaluate experiences of the sacred entails reflections on the revelation that Christians make central: Jesus the Christ. What does this state of affairs suggest for a contemporary Catholic spirituality?

Catholic theology has spoken of grace as perfecting nature. It has taught that sin does not vitiate human nature or corrupt it to the core. So while wise people check on their impulses, they do not consider their basic equipment (sensation, reason, emotion, volition) faulty. They do not assume that what looks good, appeals to common sense, creates happiness, or beckons as a value that they ought to try to achieve is probably deceptive, if not pernicious. Their assumption is that experience teaches people the difference between true and merely apparent goods, and that the Spirit of God is always working to help people of faith discern the presence of God in their experience. Insofar as people attend to the Spirit of God, they come to realize how goods other than God are relative, but also how every true good (whether material or spiritual) is a gift of God—food, children, learning, love, and all the rest.

In this horizon, any experience of the sacred that human beings confess can be salutary. Whatever seems to be especially real, true, good, or beautiful is worthy of human attention, may well be worthy of human admiration. Any aspect of human existence may reveal the sacred. Work, sex, song, study, prayer, sacrifice—seen in the right angle, experienced in the right way—all can swell up with great significance. If the historian of religion studies many different manifestations of the sacred, that is more than fitting. For the Christian doctrine about creation, each limited being, each moment, each ceremony depends on God for its existence. It is no wonder, then, that any limited being can occasion a hierophany—a manifestation of the sacred. And yet, of course, it is a wonder, because only the experience of hierophany makes the Christian doctrine of creation, or similar doctrines from other traditions, come alive and shows its full import.

Mircea Eliade believed that human beings long to live in sacredness. His studies of a great many religious ideas, rituals, histories, and the like convinced him that the report from millennial humanity was that not to live in sacredness was to suffer grievously. But no group claimed that it could always live in sacredness. Consistently the report was also that achieving harmony with a sacred cosmos, or with sacred deities, or with the realest parts of the self was an ongoing battle. Perhaps the saints came close to finding God in all things, but ordinary people did well to find God (sacredness) now and then. From this experience of our human inability to achieve the ideal came myths about falls from grace and numerous rituals designed to facilitate restoration.

The Christian interested in spirituality can take comfort from this interpretation of human history. If the overall record shows that men and women have sought union with sacredness so typically that the sacred has virtually defined their sense of themselves, then the ancient Christian notion that the soul is naturally Christian (is oriented by nature to what Christ revealed) seems verified. Philosophers, or historians of religion, no doubt could call for many distinctions, but Christian theologians are bound to think that God has indeed left traces of divinity everywhere.

But is the sacred identical with the Christian God? Is each finding of secure meaning, of apparently ultimate reality and truth, assimilable to Christ? Why not? Christians believe that there is only one God, the maker of heaven and earth. They believe that God desires the salvation of all people. And they believe that Christ died and rose once and for all, becoming the axis of the history of salvation. On Christian grounds it seems easy to argue that each experience of the sacred, which presumably is helpful to the salvation of the person to whom it occurs, is an experience of the one God and of the Christ who is the axis of the history of salvation.

When an ancient California Indian experienced the rock face in Yosemite Valley known as "El Capitan" and found it an expression of the sacred, that person experienced a reality, a goodness, a power, a beauty—call it what you will—that revealed new depths of meaning in ordinary human existence. Inasmuch as such a revelation moved the person to awe, reverence, gratitude, a desire to live a better life, and the like, the Christian has to find the grace of God at work. And because for the Christian the grace of God comes to focus through Jesus the Christ, the Christian has to think that the person's experience at "El Capitan" had a connection to Jesus the Christ.

Mircea Eliade does not make such a connection. He does not work as a Christian theologian. But he does show how strong a role experiences of the sacred have played in most traditional cultures, and he does conclude from his researches that the sacred itself is part of human consciousness—so old a feature of human awareness that it is ingredient in humanity's traditional self-understanding: "The 'sacred' is an element in the structure of consciousness and not a stage in the history of consciousness. On the most archaic levels of culture, *living, considered as being human,* is in itself a *religious act,* for food-getting, sexual life, and work have a sacramental value. In other words to be—or, rather, to become—*a man* [person] signifies being 'religious.' "[5] If we interpret Eliade benignly, then, we come to the Christian sense that nothing human is foreign to the God who took flesh in Jesus—that all decent human pursuits depend on the grace of God and reveal it.

Hermeneutics

The generation of historians of religion that has arisen after the dominance of Mircea Eliade has tended to sharpen his concern with meaning, often by calling on recent theories of hermeneutics. Understanding has become the central category in many recent works on comparative religion, where one tries to translate across cultures. Eliade himself praised this effort, advertising the work of Lawrence E. Sullivan on South American religions (which takes a hermeneutical approach) as follows: "This is an astonishing work—the most important and original *oeuvre* on religion which I have read."[6] It may profit us, then, to attend to a hermeneutical approach to the history of religions such as Sullivan's.

Early in the book to which Eliade refers Sullivan writes: "Hermeneutics is the willingness to treat the attempt at interpretation as a peculiarly instructive cultural process affected by both the subject and the object of understanding. In an authentic interpretation, one's method cannot stand objectively apart from one's data; it must become subject to the data in order adequately to grasp what one engages in the act of understanding. The process of interpretation must continually be reexamined in the light of one's attempts to understand. In this light, the up-front confession of one's method often appears simplistic and ill timed, for one cannot so quickly dispatch with the self-awareness that genuine understanding requires. The categories that assemble one's facts and the terms, procedures, and 'conclusions' that explain them must remain problematic and subject to question throughout the course of the inquiry. How do one's own forms of knowledge reshape and reveal the meaning of another's thoughts or acts, and vice versa? Understanding is a creative process, and, when it is performed well, the nature of that creativity is itself assessed in the act of interpreting culture."[7]

This is a salutary renunciation of the pretentiousness that attended some early views of hermeneutics. It owns up to the essentially dialogical character of cultural interpretation, in which the student both listens to the data of the people under consideration and, willy-nilly, reports back to such people data from his or her own cultural formation. Thus "understanding" becomes an ongoing adventure, and one cannot define with any ease how data and student, those under investigation and those investigating, stand, because any adequate depiction of their interrelations would have to be both holistic and evolving.

But how does "understanding" relate to the personal commitments of either the people studying or the people being studied? How, in other words, does scholarship, even the most hermeneutically sophisticated, relate to the mysteriousness of the human situation on both sides of the investigative equation—the mysteriousness that calls for the scholar not to postpone personal acceptance of the necessity for faith, and that illumines the ultimate motivation of the people being studied (for example, native South Americans)? In our view, fashioned from the experiences and exigencies germane to an adequate contemporary Christian spirituality, the mystery so predominates in all cases that any irreligious hermeneutic is foolish and any purely academic exegesis of the interpretational experience is superficial.

Any irreligious hermeneutic, implicit or explicit, is foolish because one cannot blink away the mystery without missing the most crucial factor in both the culture of the people one is studying and one's own consciousness. But to miss the most crucial factor—the people's bone-deep knowledge that all their myths and rituals are provisional and problematic, because none can render the ultimate meaning of their existence definitively; one's own similar awareness, when one is quiet, deep, honest—is to ruin one's study from the outset. Thus any reduction of religion to sociology, psychology, economics, or hermeneutics (in the sense of a theory that does not ground meaning in mystery) is disastrous. Nowadays, few historians of religion would propose such a reduction explicitly, but many seem to propose it implicitly, inasmuch as they do not grapple with the issue raised by John of the Cross in the text that we quoted: the privileged place that direct knowledge of God, the divine mystery, claims for itself.

It would be completely acceptable for academic scholarship to throw up its hands before this issue, claiming that every religious group is prone to exalt certain experiences as revelatory and arrange all other knowledge in terms of them, except that stopping at that point pretends that the academic investigators themselves are exempt from this rule. They are not, both because their methodological precepts tend to assume quasi-religious status (even when such precepts are as vague or rich as Sullivan's) and because the investigators remain vulnerable human beings subject to the same existential forces (death, evil, finitude, ignorance; ecstasy, love, goodness, holiness) that made the people that they study religious (tied to ultimate mystery).

So the real thrust of depictions of the hermeneutical circle such as Sullivan's, in the mind of people like ourselves who are trying to imagine a contemporary spirituality (personal pathway) both informed by the full sweep of the data offered by the history of religions and committed to Christ, is toward the functional equivalence of all the parties involved. The people whom a Sullivan studies, Sullivan himself, and Christians trying to fashion a viable spirituality all stand helpless before the existential mysteriousness of human existence.

None of us has ever seen God. All of us make do, muddle through, through commitments, leaps of faith, more or less honestly and fully acknowledged. Traditional peoples like Sullivan's South Americans are clear that their myths, their master-stories, guide their way. In these they place their hopes, more or less knowingly. Christians reflecting on the foundations of their spirituality realize that they are opting for the myth of Jesus—the master-story at the center of the New Testament and the life of the Christian community. What are historians of religion relying upon? What are their myths, the master-stories making them think that their works and lives are justifiable?

Some may rely on traditional religious options, for example Christian or Jewish faith. Others (the majority, if O'Flaherty's impression is correct) rely on an agnosticism or atheism that says that there is no preferred way of coping with ultimate mystery, no faith that will render the sacred congenial, a matter of such experience that one can call it an intimate friend, a parent, even a lover. And most, adhering to a not-so-unwritten rule of their guild, treat their work on religion as requiring them to prescind from the question of faith or non-faith—the question of how they themselves are grappling with ultimate mystery. Their argument is that personal faith is irrelevant, an argument both as winning and as fatuous as the parallel argument that whether oncologists have personally been stricken with cancer is irrelevant to the medicine that they practice. Certainly historians of religion and oncologists can tell us wonderful things about their subjects, even when those subjects have not scored their own flesh. Yet who would blame us for refusing to grant either such group real wisdom about their subjects, as long as they themselves remained unafflicted?

So, until hermeneutical sophistication about the history of religions brings scholars to incorporate the mysteriousness, and so the religiousness, of their own overall human venturing into their methodological reflections, people searching for a viable Christian spirituality are right to limit the contributions that such scholars might make. In the spiritual life, as the religions themselves regularly conceive it, there is no genuine wisdom not rooted in personal experience—indeed, in personal suffering. Scholars who range widely over the data of the history of religions can help us to contextualize our spiritual searches, but until the "understanding" that they achieve speaks in the first person about ventures that either brought them personal peace or failed to do so, exponents of a Christian spirituality will not be able to consider them fellow-travelers—people equally honest and humble about the primary human task: responding to the challenges that the divine mystery puts to each of us utterly personally.

Humanism

For several influential figures in American religious studies, the wave of the future lies with those who (a) treat religion from a humanistic point of view, and (b) are interested in particular data from a given tradition mainly for the light it sheds on general principles. Jacob Neusner and Jonathan Z. Smith are allied in this conviction, and it should prove stimulating to engage with their position.

Neusner has said of the humanistic study of religion (the kind of study that he and Smith argue should predominate in the university): "Humanistic study of a religion, or religion as a genus of human activity, asks what we learn about humanity from humanity's yearning for God, devotion to supernatural revelation, dedication of this life to the life to come, and vision of humanity as a sacred projection onto earth. The humanistic study of religion reverses matters. Compared to a theological approach it is to see divinity as a secular projection onto heaven, religion as a principal datum for the study of humanity."[8]

This is a clear statement, but it leaves hanging several crucial methodological matters. First, what is the understanding of "humanity" that humanistic scholars assume? Is humanity something that one can define apart from the self-understanding that comes to people from their encounters with divine mystery—that is, apart from the sense of self or community that many peoples have felt that divinity revealed to them? At the least, people studying the various religions ought to be sensitive to the claims that oppose any definition of humanity that is secular—any definition that does not make sacrality (which usually appears to people as a gift, something come to them from a beyond that they do not control) determinative if not constitutive.

In other words, simply to impose a secular understanding of religion (an anti-theological understanding) is to work a significant fallacy and raise questions about one's basic honesty. The view that one takes of humanity, religion, divinity, sacrality, secularity and all the other terms that are likely to become relevant ought to be laid out fully, not simply assumed or imposed. But laying this out fully would entail the kind of apologetics that becomes personal: how the given interpreter sees the world, whence he or she derives the hierarchies, the preferential options, that will guide the studies to come. Neusner makes a good case for the rich yield that a humanistic interpretation can bring, but he does not grapple adequately with the prior issue: Why is this kind of interpretation preferable to a theological one? Why is it legitimate or advantageous to bracket personal faith? Certainly, there are obvious and powerful answers that one can make to these questions, but there are also obvious and powerful counteranswers that theologians, standing for the majority of religious people throughout history, can make. Before one hustles on to project a complete program for the study of religion, one ought to deal thoroughly with these foundational issues.

Under the influence of Smith, who has worked in more traditions than he himself has, Neusner also says about the ideal study of religion: "Now, at the present state, as is clear, our effort is to find a common program of questions to address to diverse religions, that is, to ask the questions of the humanities, to discover and define religion. Our work is to treat the various religious traditions as exemplary of religion. Given religions, at a given point in their history and society, may offer interesting data to exemplify a phenomenon of religion important beyond themselves. What is important only for itself teaches mere facts. What is important beyond itself, what supplies an *e.g.,* so to speak, is what we seek in the several religious traditions before us."[9]

This reads quite well, and anyone who has suffered from positivistic historical studies will stand up and cheer. Yet it still begs several more basic questions. How are we to come to our sense of the "religion" that a given example from a given religion illumines or illustrates significantly? What is the hermeneutical circle involved in moving back and forth between the religions that offer us our data and the understanding of religion in general that we want both to emerge from our studies of the data and to give such data their significance (as examples of more profound or common principles)? Finally, there is the question that emerged from our reflections on Sullivan's hermeneutical approach: Where does the investigator's own immersion in religion (understood as our ineluctable tie to limitless mysteriousness) factor in?

The drift of our resistance to humanistic studies of religion has become plain. Since "humanistic" is regularly understood as anti-theological (or at least as arrogating the right to pass judgment on theological claims and assign them their place in a schema generated from other principles), it runs afoul of the core of a spirituality such as the Catholic one we are imagining. A spirituality such as ours takes faith as its horizon. It is theological in the classical sense that faith, a definite stance toward the mystery at the core and foundation of human existence, comes first and understanding comes second. Indeed, understanding remains in the service of faith.

Why? Because we know that understanding will always be partial, fettered, unequal to the task of engaging with the mystery in the ways necessary to find "salvation" (healing, fulfillment, meaning strong enough to defeat evil and death). Faith is as much a function of the heart as of the mind. Faith is a matter of commitment that goes beyond what we can ever justify in detail. The vast majority of human beings have been formed by traditions that gave faith priority, and even those human beings who have not been formed by such traditions remain creatures of a day pressured from all sides to love beyond what they can know.

Jonathan Z. Smith defines the project and skill of the student of religion in ways keeping with the position that he and Neusner have been developing: "For the self-conscious student of religion, no datum possesses intrinsic interest. It is of value only insofar as it can serve as *exempli gratia* of some fundamental issue in the imagination of religion. The student of religion must be able to articulate clearly why 'this' rather than 'that' was chosen as an exemplum. His primary skill is concentrated in that choice. This effort at articulate choice is all the more difficult, and hence all the more necessary, for the historian of religions who accepts neither the boundaries of the canon nor of community in constituting his intellectual domain, in providing his range of exempla."[10]

This description also has its winning notes, freeing us as it would from premature or restrictive senses of what religion can be. Yet it too leaves crucial assumptions unexplained and undefended. Is it possible to work without a canon or a community—can any scholar's choices be so free of the education and tradition in which he or she was raised (even when that education and tradition have been rejected)? And, again, what is the religion that is being exemplified well by the astute choices and exemplified badly or weakly by the less impressive? The terms we have to use in debates such as this, if we are to be radically humanistic (are to get to the mysteriousness so crucial to our sense of ourselves, our works and days), are so primitive and fundamental that anything less than a full exposition of how one understands human nature and destiny, which is sure to include a difficult examination of "God," is inadequate. Equally inadequate, in the minds of people seeking help in developing a viable spirituality, are treatments that are not personal—that will not bear the burden of putting the self on the line for the choices it has made in face of the imperatives of life's finitude, wretchedness, joy, and, above all, mysteriousness.

Personalism in Spirituality

In contrast to the detachment that many academic approaches to religion propose as ideal, Catholic spirituality of the type that we are developing is thoroughly attached—thoroughly personal. It may profit immensely from academic studies (including academic studies of spirituality),[11] but it believes that the aim of spirituality is not academic. People do not pray and labor to promote social justice so that they may write a book, teach university classes, or enlarge the fund of humanity's knowledge. They pray and labor to promote social justice because they think that this is what God wants of them. This is how they are to love the Lord, their God, with whole mind, heart, soul, and strength, and how they are to love their neighbors as they love themselves. The entire enterprise is personal, because it concerns their own salvation and fulfillment. They cannot do otherwise, because they have met the divine mystery and realized that contending with it, loving it, letting it have its way in their hearts is the very marrow of what it means to be human. From Rumi singing the plaintive song of the reed to Ignatius Loyola wanting to serve under the banner of Christ's cross, the exemplars to whom people passionate about spirituality look have not been academicians. They have been poets and lovers, people of passionate imagination, prayer, and action.

Does this mean that academic studies of religion, including of spirituality, are worthless, so that people interested in spirituality should set them aside as irrelevant? By no means. As we have insisted, knowing about the full range of humanity's religious experience can help people interested in Christian spirituality to contextualize their own venture—know something of the grid on which to place it, when they try to imagine how it relates to other people's experiences. But people actually pursuing a spiritual life have to limit the contributions and authority of academic studies if they are to retain their own focus. They have to insist that what goes on in the inner precincts of their venture is utterly existential, a personal encounter with divinity. As Thomas à Kempis put it, it is better to feel compunction than to know its definition. The people who succeed at prayer may find help in academic studies of prayer, but their greatest help will come from quiet, solitude, owning up to their sins and pouring out their hearts to their God. Similarly, the people who succeed in contributing to justice and peace may find help in reports about poverty, international arms-dealing, successful techniques for non-violent resistance, but they will learn and accomplish more by working with the poor or working against the proliferation of violence.

In saying that spirituality should be personalist, we imply that everything germane to the person has a rightful place. Thus there is a place for the body and the mind, as well as for the spirit. There is a place for communal ventures, as well as for solitary ones. Art can be very useful, but so can expertise in economics or psychology. The point is that none of these things comes into play for its own sake. In spirituality everything that the person can call upon subserves the single goal of meeting and serving God. Inasmuch as the religions could agree that this goal defines the human vocation, they could agree that spirituality serves their purposes well.

Similarly, they could agree that academic preoccupations such as the history of religions serve their purposes only partially. Because it is more holistic, spirituality is both more religious than academic preoc-cupations and more personal. Spirituality forces people to stand up and be counted. It will not tolerate the passive voice or the third person. It will not let people hide behind the supposed objectivity of detached scholarship. Always it insists that God speaks, demands, invites in the present, very concretely, in ways directly proportioned to each different interlocutor. God is not a scholar or a scientist. God does not care about professional qualifications. When it comes to spirituality, all of the qualifications are personal, idiosyncratic: the unique person's history of saying yes and no to grace.

Academic students of religion rightly ask a reprieve from this sort of personalism. In their work they do not want to have to hoist at all times the baggage of what something means to themselves or their students personally. That baggage slows up study of objective data, and accenting the personal tends to open huge areas for debate. As long as academicians remember that they are setting aside the fruit of the religious enterprise to deal with the husks, there should be no problem. Everyone knows that religious passions can inflame, and that objectivity about religion is difficult, when people from various traditions are together.

But academicians studying religion have done so well with their objective detachment, within the narrow arena that they have demarcated for measuring success, that they have tended to forget what they have set aside. Indeed, they have tended to forget that they are only human beings, called by divine mystery, before and after they are academicians. They are only human beings, people forced to faith of some sort by life itself, more centrally, more crucially, than they are scholars or teachers. Certainly our faith is so central that if we are scholars or teachers our faith marks our scholarship or teaching, and our scholarship or teaching marks our faith. But one is more significant than the other. If only because we die, our faith, by which we contend with death, willy-nilly, is obviously more significant. Death, as the most daunting reminder of the priority of divine mystery, ensures that no one be able to define himself or herself as simply a scholar, or a teacher, or a writer, or a mother, or a scientist, or a priest.

It is not hard to argue that the best theory of consciousness, and so the best methodology in religious studies, is the most personal. Michael Polanyi and Bernard Lonergan have made this argument most cogently, and each has been beautifully sophisticated about the rights and limits of the different human occupations, including scholarship and mysticism.[12] Spirituality comes out well in such cognitional theories, because spirituality is so directly the product of the person's entire effort to know and to love, to see and to act, to pray and find ultimate meaning. Scholarship also comes out well, because it is a noble employment of human reason, and human reason is a glory of humankind. But scholarship that sequesters itself from divine mystery, faith, theology, and the other existential aspects of consciousness, as religion spotlights it, does not come out well, when one examines self-understanding and methodological acumen.

The fact is that we cannot make do with short-cuts in religious studies. To be faithful to our data, both those coming from the "outside" of the various religious traditions and those coming from the "inside" of our own immersion in the mysteries that shape such traditions, we have to deal with the holistic and existential aspects of our enterprise. We cannot expect that fobbing the most crucial part of the task—what we ourselves bring to it and are making from it—off on a discredited theology and reserving the university's part of the task to humanistic approaches will play in the concert halls where people want real music, the music of the spheres.

This remains true even when the academic orthodoxy of the day shouts down anyone so presumptuous as to whisper that the emperor has no clothes—that no amount of scholarship can paper over the fact that the mystery addresses all of us personally, and that we can only separate this address from our religious studies artificially, in bad faith, because we all know, in our heart of hearts, that God allows no such separation. At the least, then, we have to explain why it is convenient, even necessary for the moment, to cordon off a sanitary zone and call it the academic study of religion—until the day, real or utopian, when all involved will be mature enough to speak fully personally: with both objectivity and subjective, passionate involvement with the divine mystery without which there is neither objectivity nor subjective passion.

Christ in Christian Spirituality

Though all spirituality, as we have defined it, is personal, Christian spirituality is personal with a vengeance, locking onto the person of Christ. Christian spirituality assumes that people have worked through the hardships of apologetics, in some fashion, so that they are committed to Christ. This does not mean that they never suffer doubts about the reasonableness of Christianity, but it does mean that, day by day, they find enough sense and beauty in the venture of loving Christ to sustain them without great trouble. Thus they are in a position to adapt findings from fields such as the history of religions to their own purposes, moving serenely, in peace and joy.

We have considered what such adaptations are likely to be, so now let us pause to sketch what the apologia for such a position of faith would be, were the committed practitioner of Christian spirituality to have the inclination, leisure, and skill to express it. It would be a frank confession that Jesus has the words of eternal life, and that no one in the given practitioner's experience has spoken as vivifyingly as he. In other words, it would be a modest self-defense: I love this man, the tradition he bequeathed to me, the experiences of sacredness that have come to me because of both. Despite all the sin and ugliness in Christian history, I find no solid reason to abandon this ship or voyage, because I know, so intimately that I could no more deny it than I could deny the color of my eyes or the line of my blood, that at specific times that I shall never forget my heart turned aglow and I was sure, for the moment, that God loved me and had purposes for me. If other people can report the same sort of experience and attribute it to other sources, that is fine. I have no quarrel with that or with them. But I find that honesty means sticking to my own actual history, which has been formed by the love of Christ. No argument no matter how academically sophisticated, no exposure to the horrors of people's inhumanity to one another, not even any stark confrontation with my own sins and worthlessness washes this conviction away. For better or worse, virtually outside of my choice, I am committed to the Christian way—and this commitment regularly sends tears of gratitude flowing down my cheeks, because of both its beauty and my unworthiness.

Most people making such a simple confession or apologia will not turn the tables on those challenging them, but if they did their speech would be equally plain: What greater beauty, pathos, depth, historical force, exact grappling with divine mystery, or moments of undeniable personal experience do you place in front of me, to suggest that I should abandon my way for another? What does your faithlessness, or scholarship, or humanism, or Buddhism, or anything else offer to compare with the cross of Christ, when it comes to epitomizing human sorrows, or to the resurrection of Christ, when it comes to coruscant hopes? You may say that my faith is childish, or illusory, or a thing for losers and the weak, but where is your manifestly superior wisdom or love? Who are you, another mere mortal, another creature of a day sure to be ignorant when it comes to the divine mystery, to convict me of folly? I have no desire to deprecate your humanism, Buddhism, or other existential pathway. I can find my God at work in every decent, noble, intelligent thing that you say or do, just as I can find my God grieving in your every suffering and hurt in your every sin. But don't look over your half-moon glasses at me, playing the superior professor, pretending to know it all, because I know that none of us knows it all—that the wisest of us, like Socrates, is the first to confess that we know most when we know how little we know, how insecure is our virtue. And if you push me too hard, breaking the bonds of my fragile virtue, I will tell you exactly what a fool you appear to be, when you pontificate or turn pridefully dismissive—what a sorry bag of *peripsema* ("offscouring," some Victorian translators of Paul blushed to render it).

Less important than any apologetic ventures, however, are the efforts of Christian seekers to turn everything toward Christ, his God, and their Spirit, because these efforts are the way that a Christian spirituality grows, not only despoiling the Egyptians properly but realizing, more and more as the years go by, how completely Christ is the one in whom all things hold together, the one through whom God, the Father, is all in all.

For a Christian spirituality rooted in a scripture such as John's gospel, all things came to be in the Word that became incarnate, and the Word's taking flesh put into creation a light that no darkness of mind or heart could ever overcome. That is the light that Christian spirituality loves. In that comprehensive, uncomprehended light, Christian spirituality finds all things holding together, whether they come from university professors of religion, eastern spiritual masters, western poets, secular heroes of resistance, or any other decent source. Grace and truth came through Jesus Christ—that is the Johannine creed. God is love, and those who abide in love abide in God, and God in them.

If we are simple believers, adherents of what C. S. Lewis once called "mere Christianity," a faith that thinks the incarnation, death, and resurrection of very God from very God enough, then these familiar words remain dynamite. Exploding from them is all the light, life, and love that human beings need, if they are not only to find satisfied the hunger ravening in their natures but also to find present a destiny they could barely accredit: divine life. And exploded by these familiar words is all the grave self-importance of the world, the flesh, and the devil—everything that puts a weight on human hope, that mocks human love, that says that to believe in a God as good as Christ's is infantile folly. Perhaps it is. Perhaps one's former friends are bound to laugh; perhaps things will become uncomfortable in the board room or at the faculty club. How laughably slight a price to pay for revelation, conversion, rapture by God's spirit. To swap the chic for the saving, the clever for the ecstatic, the superior for the self-emptying that put divinity into human limbs, gave divinity eyes of blue and brown and green— what a raw, difficult barter.

The fact is that the clever of this world are living lives of quiet desperation, that the worldly wise are haunted at midnight, when they can chatter no more and finally have to navigate silence. The fact is that they, like ourselves, feel like motherless children and long for nothing more than a mystery good enough, improbable enough, to wipe every tear from their eyes and make death be no more. Christians have no superiority over these people, least of all fundamentalist Christians, wrapped in their prideful certainties and defending themselves against divine mystery, a Word that will not be chained. These people are our sisters, our brothers, ourselves. We find them in the mirror and when we examine our consciences. We blush at all the ways in which they are better than we. But not even this matters, because now and then we recall a name, an ancient story handed down, touching on Jesus of Nazareth, the center of our spirituality. No academic discipline compares with the simple science about him available in the gospels. On every page they ask us to study him not with nimble minds or sharpened tongues, but with a steady gaze and purity of heart, willing only one thing: to know him personally, and what he wants of us.

What he wants of us does not end with the gospels. It continues to be a nagging question when we read about worthy Taoists such as Chuang Tzu, or about estimable rabbis, or about historians of religion who have unlocked treasures of humanity in cultures distant to us (but not distant to the one God or the one Logos). We should have no desire to dominate these non-Christians, just as we can make no agreement to their dominating us. We can only agree to the sorts of honest, loving exchanges that make their experiences illumine our faith, and make our experiences illumine their deepest commitments. It is for God to separate or join the various pathways, the different spiritualities, as it is for God to say, in the final analysis, which methodologies have most helped produce the images that God most treasures: saintly people standing out for goodness and wisdom.

NOTES

1. Greg Spinner and Wendy Doniger O'Flaherty, "*Other People's Myths:* An Interview with Wendy Doniger O'Flaherty," in CRITERION: A PUBLICATION OF THE DIVINITY SCHOOL OF THE UNIVERSITY OF CHICAGO, 29/1 (Winter 1990), 5–6.

2. See Bernard Lonergan, METHOD IN THEOLOGY (New York: Herder & Herder, 1972), pp. 101–124.

3. John of the Cross, *The Spiritual Canticle,* 26/13, in THE COLLECTED WORKS OF ST. JOHN OF THE CROSS, trans. Kieran Kavanaugh and Otilio Rodriguez (Washington: Institute of Carmelite Studies, 1973), pp. 513–514.

4. Mircea Eliade, A HISTORY OF RELIGIOUS IDEAS, Vol. 1 (Chicago: University of Chicago Press, 1978), p. xiii.

5. Ibid. See also Ugo Bianchi, "History of Religions," in THE ENCYCLOPEDIA OF RELIGION, ed. Mircea Eliade (New York: Macmillan, 1987), vol. 6, pp. 399–408, which surveys the different disciplinary approaches that have sheltered under the umbrella of "the history of religions" recently.

6. Mircea Eliade, in "Praise for Icanchu's Drum," on the back jacket of Lawrence E. Sullivan, ICANCHU'S DRUM (New York: Macmillan, 1988).

7. Lawrence E. Sullivan, ICANCHU'S DRUM, p. 16.

8. Jacob Neusner, "Preface," in TAKE JUDAISM, FOR EXAMPLE: STUDIES TOWARD THE COMPARISON OF RELIGIONS, ed. Jacob Neusner (Chicago: University of Chicago Press, 1983), p. xi.

9. Ibid., p. xvi.

10. Jonathan Z. Smith, quoted without textual reference by Neusner in ibid., p. x.

11. For passing comments on methodology in Christian spirituality, see the collaborative three-volume work CHRISTIAN SPIRITUALITY (New York: Crossroad, 1985, 1987, 1989) and the collaborative one-volume work THE STUDY OF SPIRITUALITY (New York: Oxford University Press, 1986). Both works are more interested in the academic study of spirituality than in our enterprise of fashioning an existential pathway rooted in Christian tradition but set in dialogue with other world religions.

12. See Michael Polanyi, PERSONAL KNOWLEDGE (New York: Harper Torchbooks, 1964), and Bernard Lonergan, INSIGHT (New York: Philosophical Library, 1958).

Chapter 7

Conclusion

The God Revealed in the History of Religions

Assuming that we have clarified, if not justified, the bent of Christian spirituality to assimilate to its own convictions data from the history of religions, let us inquire now into the senses of divinity that Christians can find when they investigate other peoples' experiences.

First, there is the numinous quality so prominent in paleolithic artifacts, which suggests that divinity has appeared not only as awesome but also as uncanny. The grotesque, provocative shapes of some numinous paleolithic figurines tell us that the ultimate powers whom our earliest forebears experienced frightened them. They could not be sure how such ultimate powers would use their sway over life and death, over good fortune and bad. So they approached such powers with fear and trembling, hoping that drawing near was wise. In the end they had no choice, because they needed desperately what the powers alone seemed to contain: fertility, health, meaning. But their religion remained filled with shadows and nightmares, as well as with sunrises and sunsets that gave them cheer. Wherever nature has been the prime deity, human beings have been ambiguous about the ultimate powers. For one could never know with nature—how one stood was never clear.

Second, the oral peoples who survived down to recent times showed that these paleolithic attitudes lingered as long as hunting and gathering (direct dependence on nature) remained the center of culture. The same interest in fertility, transition from death to life, and ecstatic sources of meaning that we can conjecture from paleolithic artifacts appears in the religious cultures of recent oral peoples. Certainly the kind of environment they have inhabited has made a significant difference, and one cannot paint all oral cultures with a single brush labeled "shamanism." But, by and large, the shamanic impulse to

161

find meaning through ecstatic travel has been prominent. Whether they symbolized this impulse in terms of surrounding spiritual forces, witchcraft, or occult healing, the native Americans, Africans, and Australians who retained oral cultures until recently all lived in a very lively spiritual universe. Their words flew, because they were not tied to writing, and in the flight of their words swarmed dozens of vivid spiritual forces, both helpful and hurtful.

If we pause to reflect on the implications that Christians might draw from this so substantial portion of human cultural history, perhaps what ought to strike us the most is the pursuit of meaning that preoccupied our longest stream of ancestors. The world over, from Asia to Europe and Africa to South America, native cultures have been far more absorbed with spirituality—meaning, harmony with the divine powers, ecstatic techniques—than they have with material technology. Yes, virtually all native peoples display some genius in adapting to their physical environments, and in controlling their social units. But the center of their cultures has been the pursuit of meaning, which they have located in experiential meetings with ultimate powers. They have thought a person filled with spiritual power rich, and they have pitied a person laid low, rendered desolate because out of sorts with the ultimate powers, no matter what that person's material possessions. Modern westerners have had many good reasons for thinking that improvements in medical care, education, and material technology would enrich native people's cultures, but too often such modern westerners have not realized how poor they themselves were, in contrast to the wealth that natives carried in their psyches. Christians interested in spirituality nowadays might take this hypothesis about recent cultural interactions between westerners and natives as a stimulus to reconsider what the core of western culture might become. How are we to revivify our own traditions, repristinate our own systems of meaning? Have the master-stories that we have told for two thousand years or more become obsolete, or do death and resurrection continue to write the basic plot of all human lives, asking us to return to our roots and bestir our symbolic creativity?

Third, the sense of divinity that predominates in the so-called higher religions of Asia (Hinduism, Buddhism, Confucianism, Taoism) is impersonal and naturalistic, correlating with a predominant veneration of the sage. If the shaman is the outstanding figure in oral cultures (including those atop which the higher Asian cultures sit), because ecstasy is the most honored way of finding sacrality and ultimate meaning, the sage is the outstanding figure in Hinduism, Buddhism, Confucianism, and Taoism.

What does the sage know? Here the traditions vary, but not so widely that they create an impossible span. Hindu and Buddhist sages know how to stop suffering, by quenching desire. They reject the passion that drives human beings to try to possess what will give pleasure, or riches, or peace, or even meaning. Confucian and Taoist sages know the rhythms of the Way, the eternal Tao that runs nature and offers human beings the path to peace. One can say that all four religious ideals traffic in detachment. The way to the Way is to travel lightly. Moreover, the way is more interior than exterior. The Chinese religions stress outer forms, ritual propriety, and the Indian religions show some equivalents (especially in Hindu ritualism). But more important is interior attunement—to the atman, to the Tao. Buddhists are the most radical, and their radicalism has made a great impact in East Asia. For their wisdom, there is no ultimate divorce between the world of suffering and ultimate reality: *samsara* and *nirvana* are one. So wisdom is knowing how to find or live by ultimacy in the midst of transiency. Wisdom is not clinging to anything, and so being able to join the dance of meaning in everything. The freedom of the sage is a condition of mind, and then of heart. The sage thinks clearly and so feels cleanly. The sage is cool rather than passionate, compassionate rather than romantic. And so the sagacious life can be very beautiful, full of physical and spiritual grace.

Christians should take many lessons from this Asian sagacity. The Ancient of Days, as Revelation speaks of the Father, seems to smile in Asian wisdom. The time of the world is very long, and this length offers human beings a liberating perspective. The purposes of God can be quite obscure, as long as one is promoting a human agenda. Christians have finally to challenge this detachment and dispassion, because their Lord was so fully engaged with human beings and so fully passionate about human suffering. But they can remember that the Father is also the Ancient of Days, running providence by a different calendar than that in Washington or the Vatican. They can remember that everything is grace, including the resurrection that confirmed the rightness of Jesus' passion.

Lastly, the God shining from testimonies of Jewish and Muslim experience is familiar to Christians because akin to what the Christian prophets have reported. Certainly, all three prophetic traditions also speak of wisdom, but they take their cue from the likes of Moses, Muhammad, and Jesus, who announced the words of a personal God, sovereign and willful. Christians are the most definite about God's love for humankind and the victory that God has worked for human history, but Jews and Muslims have nearly equal resources for thinking that their God desires intimacy. So the main lesson that Christians might draw from Jewish and Muslim history is one of humility: we are far from alone in our sense of revelation; the focus we place on the flesh of Christ can only draw greater significance from friendly comparison with Jewish and Muslim foci.

In the next section we consider modern secularism, which the history of religions has to consider, both because "the history of religions" is itself so frequently a "humanistic" (that is, secular) venture, and because secularism has become the leading alternative to traditional absorption with the sacred. The secular culture that tries to avoid, deaden, or deny the radical mysteriousness of human existence is probably the greatest enemy of real humanism nowadays. But for the moment let us pause to rejoice in the rich legacy of human dealings with sacred mystery that the history of religions suggests. Since time out of mind, men and women more like ourselves than not have faced the key questions that we face: what to base our lives upon, where to escape from the flux of time that carries us so remorselessly, how to embrace physical and moral beauty so that neither they nor we perish. Thus, from time out of mind we have all been involved in an amazing adventure, and at the privileged moments when we could share our deepest hopes and fears, we have composed what Christians are bound to call the body of Christ—the whole phylum of flesh incarnating the need for divine wisdom and deathlessness.

Current Secularism

The divinity manifested in the history of religions encourages people interested in Christian spirituality to think that always and everywhere their God has been intriguing people, luring them to intimacy. The clarifications that came with Christian revelation were precious beyond compare, but they did not introduce a new substance into the relations between human beings and divinity. From the beginning, God was loving, desiring the best for men and women. This continues to be true today, when often the problem is not the undifferentiated character of people's perceptions of God (the problem that the pre-Christian era suffered, as Christians see it) but the deadening of our sense of God (the "eclipse" of which Martin Buber spoke).

We have to qualify this statement immediately, but we should linger with it long enough to accept its challenge. The secularization that developed in modernity (from the seventeenth century in the west) gradually created an eclipse of God from high culture. Peasants might continue to sense the sacrality of the land and the seasons, but people inhabiting such characteristically new human creations as factories and urban sprawl lost this sense. Machines and noise ousted the God who had come in handcrafts and pastoral quiet. Relations with family members and neighbors attenuated. Uprooted from the land, and split from kith and kin, many people felt quite lost. Frequently their faith went the way of their sense of belonging. When they no longer loved a particular spot of land and a particular circle of familiar friends, they did not know how they stood with God.

Naturally, modern history is more complicated than this, but most analysts of secularism—the sense that this-world is all that matters—find social uprootings very important. The intellectuals who were persuaded by a new philosophical understanding of physical science that there was no need for God remained a minority. The great masses of people who found their religious lives troubled were victims of social dysfunctions—ways that families, places of work, schools, churches, and the other key institutions of their lives no longer projected a hospitable universe.

One can say that God has always lived or died by people's individual sense of interiority, which no social shifts can take away, but this is at best a half-truth. All of us live amid swirls of culture, popular or higher, and these swirls are bound to influence us. When the imagery that they project does not depict nature as the body of God, or the church as the body of Christ, or human interiority as a stillness touched by God, none of us are as peaceful, as joyous, as we might be.

People writing about Christian spirituality often contend with various aspects of secularism vigorously, showing how art and creative science, parenting and friendship, sexual love and prayer continue to mediate experiences of the sacred. They also show that if we are pained by secular torpor, worried that our lives make no sense, guilty because we sense we ought to be single-minded but find we cannot be, we manifest our need of God in a negative mode, but a real one nonetheless: it would not hurt us to miss God if we had not been made for God.

The spiritual life is the life that searches for meaning, reality, true value. As Eliade found from countless testimonies, the sacred is what redeems the profane, the merely factual. To live in mere factuality, in an horizon of here-and-now, is to live in a cultural prison. To have no counter to the endless sweep of history, which carries everything to the morgue, is to risk madness. Human consciousness is made for transcendence. Always we want and need to go beyond where we now find ourselves, to commune with a reality that we cannot corrupt. So human consciousness is innately religious, even when buying and selling, hustling and prostituting, seem to have taken it over and established a tyranny.

In this book we authors have bitten the hand of the history of religions on occasion, because sometimes it has seemed to be feeding us stale goods out of secular stores. What it has said about humanity's religious experience has been splendid, immensely useful, but how it has qualified its presentations or stipulated that we ought to use these data has been repressed, even retarded. The proper response to the adventure played out in humanity's creations is awe, and then worship of the creator of such rich diversity and holiness. No healthy spirit could witness such testimony to the human hunger for God and sense of having been found by God without bowing low, desiring with all its strength to go and do likewise. So when historians of religion have tried to tame the impact of their data, tried to restrict significance to the level of talk and interesting ideas, they have manifested a significant disease.

The disease is secularism, and yet to discern it correctly we have to admit that it sprang from much diseased religion. Genuine religion is the champion of truth, creativity, and love, not their enemy. Genuine religion wants no authority but that earned by love and service, so it cannot be tyrannical. Many of the moderns who revolted against traditional religion met inauthentic versions. Those professing to speak in the name of God cared more about law and order than about truth, more about power than about love. Even when one can sympathize with their assessments of what the common people needed, if they were to live in stable situations, one has to lament the lack of living contact with the primordial mysteriousness of God that caused such authorities to botch their historical moment so badly.

Still, even though it is understandable that many people revolted against premodern religion, with its stress on a God beyond the world and a heaven to come, the secularism that these people fostered turned out to be poor rations. Humanism, social justice, the emancipation of the mind and the lower classes—splendid in themselves, when they became passions that bid to supply for traditional religion, they could not do the job. Nothing but God can.

That is the clear lesson of secularism, even though billions have yet to learn it. Horrible as fundamentalism is, one can sympathize with fundamentalists who think that they have no other alternative to secular meaninglessness. Rather than tolerate more political corruption, or mindless consumerism, or ceaseless warfare, or narcotics, they set out to find the sacred, the really real, the holy. The pity is that they, too, win only such a half-loaf, not finding the real Lord of the worlds, the true creator from nothingness. With time, one can pray, they may find the right path, the one of those whom Allah has favored.

For our Catholic spirituality, the full way to life and vigor is to find the living God of the Christian tradition in prayer and serve that God in good works geared to the needs of one's suffering neighbors. The full way is to draw from and contribute to a community of disciples that does not seclude itself from the world but gambles that God is the depth and beauty of every good thing or moment it encounters. We shall develop these thoughts in the next sections, but here we should acknowledge a debt to secular American culture. By its very superficiality, in the university as well as outside, it has forced us to dig deeper than we might have, and so to have learned more about the real God. Had we lived in a culture that knew even the abc's of the spiritual life (contemplation, detachment, the primacy of selfless love), we might have slugged along. Since we did not, we had to imitate Lao Tzu: shut the doors of the television cabinet, withdraw to the desert of interiority and tradition, be still and learn that only God is God.

Compassion

The sufferings of our fellow human beings, both those who lived long ago and those afflicted by present-day secularism, stand out more impressively, when we learn that only God is God. When we feel that the crucified Christ is our most precious index of God, such sufferings become sacramental. The food that Christ gave for the life of the world was his own flesh. The flesh that any human beings give over to God, in trust that their lives will finally find redemption, can be daily food for our Christian spirituality.

Our ordinary human flesh, so vulnerable, is our greatest bond. If any of us is pricked, he or she will bleed. It does not matter that we come from a despised ethnic or religious group, that we are usurers, even that we think ourselves exceptional. Our flesh gives all notions of singularity the lie. As we have evolved, through God's providential oversight, cancer can strike any of us down, earthquakes are horrible wherever they occur. To be a parent, in any part of the globe, is to worry about vulnerable children. To be hungry is to worry about how one will survive, and about the justice of life. We are one, when it comes to the bedrock realities of human existence. Suffering sweeps away almost all of our diversity. And so suffering stands against us as the fiercest witness to our folly, when we persist in hating one another, or when we will not cooperate to make a decent world. Once again, Christians should find it remarkable that their icon of God suffered so dramatically. As well, they should find it remarkable that Christ is so little an accuser, so much more a savior and friend.

The pathos that human history reveals, including the pathos of the spiritual sufferings of people who think they have thrown off religion, is a mainspring of significant spirituality. When people are moved to the center of their beings, like the biblical God moved to her womb, they are primed to fulfill the second great commandment and love their neighbors as they love themselves. One of our greatest problems is the matter of scale. When we let the pathos of real neighbors affect us, we find it easy to respond with all the help we can muster. But the millions of unreal neighbors whom we meet only through the news media cannot affect us so powerfully. Our circuits overload, and we feel helpless, because our resources are so puny. So we carry the weight of a bad conscience, and we wish that we did not have to read the newspaper. If we are honest, we admit that we pray that God will absolve us of our callousness.

Such absolution is between us and God, of course, so outsiders, even spiritual directors, can never know fully how it is going. What have we done with the talents that God gave us, including the gifts of sensitivity to suffering? The more that we translate the Pauline question of righteousness into terms such as these, the more we understand why the apostle said that no one could be sure of standing approved by God. All of us can, have to, believe that God is inclined to approve us, because of God's own goodness, but none of us could pass inspection in God's court of law.

The sufferings of the world that push people to work for social justice are the sufferings of God's people. There is no distinction between the children whom God accepts in the name of Christ and other children. They constitute one family. God loves them all, without exception. So when we represent them before God, at our prayers of petition, we are not representing strangers. Each one of the 5.5 billion people on the earth today has a direct tie to Christ, a direct claim upon the Father whom Christ served. Certainly such a statement depends wholly on Christian faith. Equally certainly, however, if one traces the different conceptual threads, one finds that it could not be otherwise. Unless the fate of all human beings is linked with Christ, there is no place in human history where one can speak of a definitive savior, an eschatological victory, a universal love that offers everyone divine life. The comprehensiveness of Christ only matches the comprehensiveness of human need. The suffering that Christ transformed is only the suffering bringing each human existence into crisis.

We cannot understand why human beings have to suffer. We can barely understand that they all do. And, accepting that they all do, now and then we can find some profit in this necessity. For example, many people, famous and ordinary, have reported that their sufferings opened their eyes, turned them around. They may say that they had to hit rock bottom before they could find their way. Or they may say that they had to lose their pride before they could appreciate the gratuity of salvation. The world itself is a gratuity, when one realizes that it did not have to be, that creatures like ourselves have never had any basis for demanding that God make them. The beauty of the world fills out when one realizes that it is completely a gift, and the suffering of the world comes into better focus: since we did not make the world, we cannot demand that it run to our ticker.

The Lord gives, and the Lord takes away—blessed be the Lord. That was the wisdom to which Job's sufferings brought him, and even though God encouraged Job to vent his frustrations, Job finds no better response. Certainly there is the problem of opposing human injustices. Certainly the liberation theologians are right to dissociate God from poverty, illiteracy, sickness, and heartache that stem from human fraud, violence, and other forms of corruption. But even in the suffering that we human beings could remove, were we to be honest and do what is decent, the purposes of God continue to work. Even there, it continues to be God who gives and God who takes away, when one gets to the ultimate shape of things. God is responsible for creation, even its dimensions of thought and freedom, where human agents are also responsible. God is the one who has to make all things well, if God is to be godly. So, in the final analysis, our very vulnerability as a species places us in the arms of God. There is no one else who can comfort us, when we have seen through all the other powers. No one else has the words of eternal life.

People who do not flee from suffering, whether its form be noble or ignoble, position themselves to hear the words of eternal life. It does not matter whether they want those words to come, or whether they dislike comings that carry religious packaging. The darkness, the silence, do what they will, regardless of our superficial wishes. We are led by ways that we would not have chosen, and we give up more of our own will than we could have imagined. At the least, we are aging, dying, realizing that soon we shall have to let go. We have not produced the successes we expected, the mark we hoped, the righteous relationship with God. We have not loved Christ as we wanted, and yet he remains knocking at the door.

A Christian spirituality has only to see the fellowship carried in human pathos, physical and emotional alike, to know how to make itself universal. Any light that another religious tradition sheds on this pathos and fellowship is catholic—useful to the whole race of us jugglers for God. God is our question and our comfort, whether we realize it or not, whether we are glad to hear it or not. We cannot get away from God. God is like a hound of heaven, pursuing us down the nights and days until we own up to what was inevitable. Inevitably we realize that our existence is much greater than we. We do not explain ourselves, least of all in our suffering. So we do not belong to ourselves. Deeper than any mark of our own, any character that we put into our souls, is the mark of God, the image of the Trinity. If we are honest, we can no more resent this not owning ourselves than we can resent not owning the wind. The wind breathes where it wishes. God can do with us what God wishes, and our wisdom is to make what God wishes our own.

Christ and Prayer

The history of religions is eloquent about the search of human beings to conform themselves to the divine will. Realizing that they could not defeat the ultimate mysteriousness, that they would have to bow in the end and so ought to bow sooner, myriad men and women became habitués of silence, brooding, praise of the sun and delight in the moon. The primordial therapy for the wounded human condition has been communion with the fullness, the foundation, that human beings knew they could never master. When they reconciled themselves to this fullness, this foundation, they usually gained peace. The measure of their lives lay out of their hands. The meaning of their time was bound to escape them. So they had to trust that their time had a purpose, that their measure would be acceptable. They had to head into death knowing that they would never know, and hoping that this nescience was good.

Christian spirituality looks on this historical necessity with compassion, because Christ has not changed our essential proportions. The necessity of submitting oneself to the divine mystery remains in force. To be sure, the revelation of divine love that streams from the side of Christ is a great benefit, making it easier to brave the darkness. But our journey continues to be by faith, rather than vision. We continue to have to surrender our lives into a dark night. If we receive unexpected consolations now and then, we have more reasons to keep surrendering, but in the final analysis God does not remove the cup of faith. The blessed equality of human existence is that we all die having to hope that we have done well, that our final fate will be fortunate. The more we can identify ourselves with Christ, who was wholly pleasing to the Father, the better we shall feel, but even this identification is more God's doing than our own.

This kind of language is what one meets in living spiritual reflection and witness. It is personal rather than impersonal, existential rather than academic. And it bears the marks of frustration, because no matter how long it goes on, it knows it can never render the mystery that is provoking it. The mystery is simple and whole, while even the best spiritual language is partial, discrete. The mystery comes into focus and fades out, while the language keeps plowing a narrow range of inspiration. Therefore much spiritual practice lets go of talking, even of thinking, to do or be as simply as possible. Indeed, much spiritual practice boils down to loving, however unsatisfying or imperfect that sounds.

What has changed since the classical ages of Christian faith, when religious practice and language occasioned little self-consciousness, is the realization that many traditions have sponsored vibrant spiritualities, and that many good people are put off by traditional piety, because they find no rootage for it in their own lives. So our project to engage the history of religions has been a chance to ventilate some Christian assumptions that have grown musty, for lack of space. In the perspective of humanity's history of searching for God, we find so many different movements of prayer, so many different struggles to do what is right, that any tradition's provincialism is detonated. Then it may be clear that searching for God, contemplating the divine mystery, is connatural—something that all people do when they receive the grace to "come to themselves" and glimpse the true proportions of their human condition. The esperanto in which human beings express this reception of grace tends to be silence. For once they shut their mouths, cool their brains, and simply attend. Feeling a lure toward solitude, wanting to abide with the relief, the peace, the new possibility that just might be coming to birth in their spirits, they become like the Madonna: recollected, reverent toward a growing mystery.

The Christian interpretation of this widespread contemplative experience is the beautiful words of Christ: "The kingdom of God is in your midst." God is not far above us and beyond our reach. God has become one with us, a full partaker of our situation and destiny. In the work of Jesus, the hunger of Jesus, the sweat of Jesus, divinity proved that it had pitched its tent in our lot. In the prayer of Jesus, God showed us how to pray—with what confidence and intimacy.

The mystery that surrounds us, as Jesus portrays it, could not be more for us, on our side. The best that any of our forebears glimpsed or hoped, Jesus assures us is so. Because they are committed to Jesus for their final interpretation of human experience, Christians can rejoice day and night. The impossible has become possible, indeed has become actual. The mysteriousness is the presence of the one God, the perfect community, the knowing and loving that have no limit or cease. The Johannine texts are the clearest: If we abide in the mystery, trust in the love, give ourselves to the light that seems to us darkness, there will be a community between us and God. We shall partake of divine life, which is deathless. What God is we shall become—not simply then, at the end of days, but right now, in the fullness of time.

The Johannine language had a prehistory and a contemporary context. But that need not render it long ago and far away. We still know what love means, what abiding means, how people who are in love abide in one another. We still sense that love wants to outpace death, and that the love responsible for the world, explaining the world's creation, must be stronger than death. And we can still catch overtones of the high priestly prayer (Jn 14–17) in which the Johannine Jesus poured out the images of his life of union with God—the life of union that he wanted his followers, his friends, to share.

So the goal, the trick, the grace is to make the mysteriousness that one finds running through the entire history of religions intimately loving. The goal is to turn the enfleshment of the Logos to such good account that we can trust that what holds the world in being bears itself toward us like a prodigal father, a nursing mother. We have the warrant to hope that the groans at the bottom of our spirits are the prayer of God the Spirit, taking all that we have, all that we want, all that we are back to God, from whom we came. The bottom of our spirits passes beyond our sight, but it does not pass beyond the reach of God. The Spirit, our advocate, prays for us better than we know, enabling us to bear the mystery. We know that we cannot see God and live. We know that beholding the mystery unveiled would destroy us. So we must let the Spirit guide us through darkness, lead us by faith, sustain us with a love too simple for us to mar.

Spirituality is bound to turn mystical like this, because God is always a mystery. And yet the mystery of God, and so the best spirituality, is utterly realistic. It does not obscure the way things are, in the real world, to make the mysteriousness, the unknowability, of human existence primary. It builds one's house on the most solid rock. The obscurantists are those who say that we can know how to price a life, the pleasures or powers for which to sell our souls. The people in flight from reality are the ones who will not abide with the mystery, will not test the proposition that God is love. Like us, they are made for contemplation and trying to do right by their neighbors. We have no natural advantage over them. If we have any special grace, it is to have been struck so forcibly by language like the Johannine, by icons of Christ, by liturgical prayer, or by the lives of the saints that we once paid attention to, did not flee. And so that is the prayer we find ourselves making: help us to keep faith with what we have been shown; keep us from fleeing. Most of our fellow-travelers in the spiritual life, eastern or western, have understood this prayer. Indeed, most have made it their own.

Index